DASSONVILLE

DASSONVILLE

William E. Dassonville, California Photographer

[1879–1957]

Researched & Edited
by
Susan Herzig
AND
Paul Hertzmann

Essay by
Peter Palmquist

CARL MAUTZ PUBLISHING
NEVADA CITY 1999

First Edition

COPYRIGHT 1999 CARL MAUTZ PUBLISHING.

ALL RIGHTS RESERVED. NO PART OF THIS PUBLICATION MAY BE TRANSMITTED IN ANY FORM OR BY ANY MEANS, ELECTRONIC OR MECHANICAL, INCLUDING, PRINTING, PHOTOCOPY, RECORDING OR ANY STORAGE AND RETRIEVAL SYSTEM, WITHOUT THE PRIOR WRITTEN PERMISSION OF THE PUBLISHER.

PRINTED IN HONG KONG.

LIBRARY OF CONGRESS CATALOG CARD NUMBER: 99-070537

CATALOGING-IN-PUBLICATION DATA

Palmquist, Peter E.
    Dassonville: William E. Dassonville,
California photographer 1879–1957 / essay by
Peter Palmquist; edited and researched by
Susan Herzig and Paul Hertzmann. – 1st ed.
  p. cm.
Includes bibliographical references and index.
ISBN: 1-887694-15-3 paper
     1-887694-16-1 cloth

1. Dassonville, William E., 1879–1957.
2. Photographers – California – Biography.
3. California – Pictorial works. I. Title

TR140.D37P35 1999   770.92 [B]
                    QBI99-571

FRONTISPIECE: William E. Dassonville, *Dunes, Carmel*. Autochrome, ca. 1910. Courtesy of the Dassonville Trust.

CARL MAUTZ PUBLISHING
228 COMMERCIAL STREET, NO. 522
NEVADA CITY, CALIFORNIA 95959
TELEPHONE 530 478-1610 FAX 530 478-0466

PAUL M. HERTZMANN, INC.
P.O. BOX 40447
SAN FRANCISCO, CALIFORNIA 94140
TELEPHONE 415 626-2677 FAX 415 552-4160

Contents

Preface
7

William E. Dassonville: An Appreciation
Essay by Peter Palmquist
9

Notes
30

Plates
33

Appendices
81

Dassonville: Exhibition History
82

Dassonville: Published Photographs
87

Dassonville: Published Articles
91

Selected Bibliography
105

Index
107

Preface

Susan Herzig
Paul Hertzmann

By 1888 when George Eastman introduced the Kodak camera, and said "you press the button, we do the rest," photography had already mustered a remarkable history of artistic achievement. There were many fine role models and an extensive body of literature. Then, pehaps more than now, photographers had great control of their medium. They sensitized their own papers, they manipulated their chemicals, they experimented constantly with combinations of science and art to evoke their feelings and express their artistic intentions. Awakening and expanding audiences for photography crowded into exhibitions to see and admire their work. The public's first opportunity to see a William Dassonville photograph was in 1900.

Our first opportunity to see a William Dassonville photograph came in January, 1977, when the San Francisco Museum of Modern Art presented seventeen early twentieth century California photographers in its retrospective, "California Pictorialism." There were eighteen Dassonvilles on the walls and one on the cover of the catalogue – a few tantalizing clues to a hidden body of work. This influential exhibition of California art photography sought to "recall ... the era of photography that had as its principal purpose the expression of forms of beauty."* It directed the gaze of viewers toward overlooked photographers and nourished a growing interest in pictorialism. Despite the positive reception, Dassonville's photographs would remain buried for another twenty years.

In the spring of 1997 we located Donald Dassonville. He invited us to share his father's legacy, stored away in two large trunks. Our first look into these trunks revealed numerous gray envelopes filled with many unknown pictures. The platinum prints were awash in a palette of silvery grays. The gum bichromates glowed on their translucent tissues, as if light shined from within. Many of the photographs were silver prints on Dassonville's famous Charcoal Black paper. This product, on which he staked his career in the second half of his life, turned out to be not one but many papers of different weights, colors, and textures, all sensitized with his secret emulsion.

From this fortunate meeting with Donald Dassonville through the research and preparation of this book, we relied upon the help of many colleagues, collectors, curators and others with a wide knowledge of art and photography. The cooperation and enthusiasm of Donald Dassonville was catalytic. We were particularly dependent on the ingenuity and research skills of Paula Freedman, whose efforts uncovered much unknown information. Michael Wilson's support and passion for pictorial photography was invaluable. Other pieces of the puzzle fit together with the help of Mary Alinder, Joseph Bellows, Katherine Crum, Elizabeth Daniels, Susan Ehrens, Andrew Eskind, Violet Hamilton, Anne Hammond and Mike Weaver, Charles Issacs, Toby Juravics, Nora Kabat, Janice Madhu, David Margolis and Jean Moss, Phiz Mezey, Merrily & Tony Page, Christian Peterson, Mike Pincus and Betsy Benford, Nancy and Peter Pool, Pam Roberts, Heather Rothaus, Amy Rule, Karen Sinsheimer, Beth Gates Warren, and Stephen White.

We would especially like to thank Peter Palmquist for sharing with us his great talent and encyclopedic knowledge of California photography and for his informative essay.

*Mann, Margery, foreword, p. 3, in the catalogue, *California Pictorialism*, San Francisco: San Francisco Museum of Modern Art, 1977.

FIGURE 1. *Portrait of William Dassonville, ca. 1905* by Arnold Genthe, reproduced in Camera Craft, *Vol. 31, No. 10, October, 1924.*

WILLIAM E. DASSONVILLE: An Appreciation

The same sun shines upon the same earth, yet each of us casts a different shadow.
W. E. Dassonville, 1902

[Dassonville's] *work, his art, is more than a business with him. It is his pleasure, his life work, and it is his desire to make each and every photograph and portrait a work of the highest standard of Art excellence.*
Thomas Dreier, Character *magazine*, 1914

Essay by Peter Palmquist

THE FABRIC woven from the threads of a man's life experiences is seldom seamless or without blemish. This is certainly true of William Edward Dassonville – artist/photographer, stubborn perfectionist and a heralded-yet-failed entrepreneur. All but forgotten today, Dassonville's photographic legacy is considerable, including an outstanding body of fine photographs in the pictorialist tradition. He was also an innovative craftsman and self-taught chemist, and a perfectionist who developed and marketed his own line of photographic printing paper: Charcoal Black. The paper was prized by the most demanding photographers, among them Ansel Adams, who later lamented that he never again "found a paper that had the particular qualities of Dassonville's Charcoal Black."[1]

In the first decade of the twentieth century, the young Dassonville rapidly gained national and international acclaim as a fine portraitist and interpreter of the California landscape. His success led to friendships with prominent figures in both commerce and art, including some of California's finest landscape painters such as William Keith. He hobnobbed with naturalist John Muir and corresponded with photographer Alvin Langdon Coburn.[2] He was sought after for portraits and many well-known American cultural figures sat for him, including Maynard Dixon, Ina Coolbrith, and John Burroughs. Reknowned type designer Frederic Goudy sought to reproduce his portrait by Dassonville as a photogravure (Fig. 2). Dassonville's work was published frequently in the United States, and as far away as England in the prestigious journal, *Photograms of the Year*. He participated in the California Camera Club as one of its most active and respected members and was associated with California's Arts and Crafts movement.

Although he was outwardly successful, with useful ideas and philosophies for others, his personal life was troubled. He had one sibling, a sister Georgia, but they had no contact as adults. His marriage failed and he became estranged from his daughter, Marion, who along with her mother, blamed him for sinking all of their money into an unprofitable business. His son Donald remembers him as a man of "tremendous fortitude and perseverance" and "a lot of patience." Donald also described him as "a very sociable person," who got along well with children and became a Boy Scout leader (but not of his own son's troop). Perhaps most telling was

FIGURE 2.
Letter dated October 25, 1915, from Frederic W. Goudy (1865-1947), prominent American type designer and printer who was aligned with the Arts & Crafts movement in America.

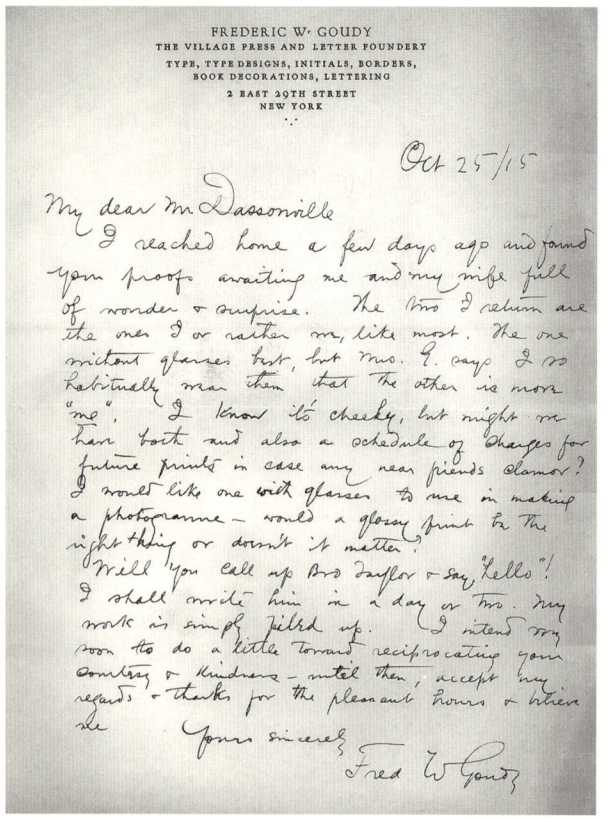

Dassonville's total disdain for taking family photographs: "He had an aversion to snap shots. Basically they are a mess, the light is wrong, the shadows are wrong, the compositions are a mess."[3]

Even his personal philosophy for photography was contradictory. Although he energetically embraced the concept of photography as art and regularly entered his own work in pictorial salons, he steadfastly refused to consider himself an artist: he was a photographer, nothing more. Nonetheless, his credo remained inexorably linked to an extreme preoccupation with things artistic. In 1902, for instance, he wrote a heartfelt article entitled, "Individuality in Photography," published in the October issue of *Overland Monthly*.[4]

He staunchly maintained that "Art is an expression, and the highest form of this expression must emanate solely from the individual," and any idea manifested from the "standpoint of art should be to give an outward form to an inward emotion."[5] Dassonville, while unwilling to don the mantle of an artist, spent most of his life providing his clients and admirers with an outward form to an inward emotion.

William Edward Dassonville was born on June 20, 1879, in Sacramento, California. His parents were Frederick Dassonville (1842–1857) and Elizabeth A. Wood (1850–?). When they married in December 1870, Frederick was age twenty-eight, a widower; his bride was age twenty. (The family name originated in Department Var in southern France, and was spelled d'Assonville.) By the mid-1880s, Frederick had moved his family to San Francisco where he was the general manager of Baker & Hamilton, dealers in wholesale hardware. Details of young Dassonville's schooling are sparse but it is known that he attended Trinity School, a fine private academy for boys. Because of his father's business connections, many of his boyhood associates were the children of merchants, including his closest friend, Fred Woods. As teenagers, the two traveled many times by river boat to Sacramento, where they obtained horses and journeyed to the town of Truckee and the Sierra Nevada for the summer months (Fig. 3).[6]

Dassonville was given his first camera as a youth and used it to photograph friends and relatives. He also packed his camera with him during his summer jaunts into the Sierra Nevada. Sometime before 1900 he joined the California Camera Club. Founded on March 18, 1890, this organization was very visible in the San Francisco artistic community. It held regular lectures, outings, and exhibitions, such as the June 27, 1890, lantern slide exhibition, "Through Japan with a Camera," attended by some 1,700 people and held in the Odd Fellow's Hall to accommodate the large crowd.

One mission of the club was to assist members in developing their photographic skills. In 1897, for example, Professor Oscar V. Lange demonstrated combination printing using 11 x 14 inch negatives. Dr. E. G. Eisen (club librarian), and others, were usually available to assist a beginning camera enthusiast. Oscar Maurer was another up-and-coming member of the club, and Arnold Genthe and Anne Brigman were closely connected as well.

Camera Craft was the official magazine of the California Camera Club, and Dassonville's membership in the organization is first confirmed in Volume 1, Number 1, May 1900. His essay, "Platinotype Printing" (Appendix, p. 91), appeared on page 29. In this essay he reveals an easy grasp of technical matters and a surprising level of self-confidence. His earliest known published photographs, "Calves" and "In the Land Fog" were also reproduced, and a brief article in this issue notes that he had recently exhibited a number of platinotype prints at an Alameda Camera Club show, "ending April 7th, and [which] was a success in every way."[7]

His growing achievements were marked by the announcement in December 1900, that he and Oscar Maurer had "joined forces" to open a portrait studio in the rear of Lassen & Bien's photographic supply house on Stockton Street. Maurer was eight years older than Dassonville, the senior partner in the new enterprise. This same notice mentioned that Dassonville had been in the employ of H. B. Hosmer "for many years" and was "one of the most skilled process workers we have on the Pacific Coast."[8] His former employer, Harrie B. Hosmer, was also a fine photographer, serving as president of the California Camera Club in 1892, and on various club committees as well. Hosmer's photographic supply store on Market Street was presumably the same site where young Dassonville gained his first-hand experience in photographic techniques.

The new studio was situated on a second floor balcony and was outfitted with "top lights opening from a light well in the center of the building." While their commercial motives are uncertain, both men continued to produce art photographs, primarily landscapes and seascapes. They also joined with other members of the California Camera Club in sending photographs for exhibition to the rooms of the prestigious New York Camera Club. Among this select group were Arnold Genthe, Laura Adams Armer, and the ever-present critic/essayist and photographer, Dr. H. D'Arcy Power.[9]

Preparations were underway for the First San Francisco Photographic Salon to be held at the Mark Hopkins Institute

FIGURE 3.
A young William Dassonville (seated on boulder) ca. 1891 with Harry Gribbes in the Sierra Nevada.

(later renamed the San Francisco Art Institute) for two weeks commencing Thursday, January 17, 1901. To be accepted, photographs had to be of high "artistic merit combined with pictorial interest." Participants could submit work in one of seven categories: Landscape, Marine, Genre, Portraiture, Still Life, Animal Studies, and Architecture including interiors. Dassonville submitted eleven entries, all landscapes. Although he failed to win a prize, his "Morning Lights" was published in the accompanying catalogue. This print and other Dassonville photographs were particularly noted by Archibald Treat in his critique, "Important Lessons of the First Salon," published in the February 1901 *Camera Craft*. Dassonville was criticized for the limited themes he presented, but Treat tactfully added, "Yet Dassonville has very original ideas, and we must expect great things from him."[10]

In the spring of 1901, Dassonville participated in the California Camera Club Exhibition of Industrial Arts held at the Mechanics' Institute Pavilion, April 17–30. As this show closed, Maurer and Dassonville, "two of the best-known San Francisco photographers," announced their intention to leave the city and travel to Paris, "where they will open a studio."[11] While it is clear that they did travel to Europe, there is no evidence that they ever set up shop in Paris. Dassonville (and probably Maurer, as well) also visited Holland where he became enamored of the Dutch landscape, a subject which quickly entered his visual vocabulary. By the close of 1901, Dassonville had returned from his European adventure and immediately joined with Henry C. Lassen in opening a new studio in the Flood Building. Oscar Maurer, apparently returning from Paris independently from Dassonville, opened his own facility at 139 Stockton Street.

Dassonville entered fourteen platinum prints in the Second San Francisco Salon (1902) including some of his Dutch landscapes which critics praised as a "vast improvement over his work of last year ... there is a clearer note in his pictures," and several portraits which were deemed "full of strength."[12] Another entry, one of the few female nudes Dassonville is known to have made, was illustrated in the catalogue of the 1902 Salon. The second Salon exhibited as well, works by some of the more famous members of the Photo-Secession, notably Alvin Langdon Coburn, F. Holland Day and Frank Eugene.

The Starr King Fraternity Second Annual Exhibition of Fine Art also hung Dassonville's work that year. As usual, many of his co-exhibitors were prominent associates from the California Camera Club. Collectively, these exhibitors challenged and encouraged each other to greater achievements. Although photography exhibitions on the West Coast took place as far back as the 1850s, these early twentieth century salons for fine-art photography garnered far greater attention from public and press than their predecessors. Dassonville's rapidly acquired reputation was a direct outgrowth of the growing attention being paid to fine-art photography.

In May at the First Los Angeles Photographic Salon, Dassonville posted two photographs. He sent only two prints since he was opening his first one-man show during that time. Under the auspices of San Francisco booksellers Paul Elder and Morgan Sheppard, Dassonville's best work was exhibited on their walls from May 22 to June 9. The show was composed "principally of portraits of children and a number of Dutch landscapes," all of the negatives dating from his recent trip to Europe.[13]

It was against this heady backdrop of exhibition and discourse concerning photography in the fine arts, that Dassonville wrote his treatise on "Individuality in Photography." (Appendix, p. 91) This essay provides our best insight into

Dassonville's persona and his views on the art of photography. Although overly earnest, his arguments are well-stated and confident. Of landscape photography he wrote, "One who wishes to interpret nature must first go to nature and learn her forms and moods; then, when he has learned this, he recreates her until she reaches his ideal of an harmonious whole." His stance on portrait work was equally perceptive:

> *In portrait photography there are two individualities to be considered – the photographer's and that of the person being photographed. Both should be considered, but this is too seldom the case with some workers who have individualized themselves, and whose work is so strongly stamped with their own individuality as to entirely obliterate that of the person being photographed.*[14]

Like many others won over to the "new school" of art photography (by which he meant the Photo-Secession), Dassonville now took an unequivocal stand that photography was an art form. He pointed out, "The work of the greatest photographers such as Demachy, Steichen, Kasebier, White and others, has been acknowledged by painters who are artists to be works of art." Distrusting the merely technical in photography, he explained, "To go to a photographer for information is to become deeply entangled in the web of error," and proposed that photographers "work entirely by themselves until they have mastered the mechanical side," and then turn to master painters "for their criticisms." He concluded his thesis with the following advice – essentially a reprise of his own creative process –"A beginner would do well not to be bound by inherited ideas, but to think for himself, for herein rests his individuality."[15]

The Third San Francisco Photographic Salon in 1903 was reviewed by the outspoken Arnold Genthe, one of the most celebrated and authoritative voices of the West Coast photographic fraternity. Of Dassonville's five entries, he preferred "No. 49 – Margaret," calling it one of the very best in the exhibition: "It depicts the unconscious charm of girlhood in a truly fascinating manner." Genthe also praised Dassonville's landscape entries as "decidedly original." His closing remark was directed at Dassonville's technical ability in printing photographs, observing that the work was done "with good taste and rare skill."[16] This was high praise indeed and was made even sweeter because the third Salon had accepted only 175 entries out of 900 submitted – stringent standards compared to the previous salon in which nearly one-half of the submitted photographs were hung.

The third Salon was enriched by the unique loan of photographs from Alfred Stieglitz, founder of the Photo-Secession. There were sixty-three prints in this group, encompassing works by all of the principal photographers that Dassonville admired. Photographs by Stieglitz, Clarence H. White, Gertrude Kasebier, Alvin Langdon Coburn and others, provided a rare opportunity to see the art of some of the finest and most acclaimed photographers in America.

Perhaps Coburn personally visited the exhibition. The two young photographers certainly met, for Dassonville made a series of striking portraits of Coburn, and one appeared as the frontispiece of the September 1904 issue of *Camera Craft*. A friendship must have sprung up between them as well. Several personal notes and invitations from Coburn were found among Dassonville's papers, including an invitation to Coburn's exhibition at the Blanchard Gallery, Los Angeles in February 1912. "Wish that you might see my exhibition .... I believe that my work has changed some in the past years since we last met and that it will interest you (Fig. 4)." Later that year Dassonville received an invitation to the wedding of Coburn and Edith Wightiana.[17]

Dassonville's peers were quick to acknowledge his talents. In July 1904, he became secretary of the California

FIGURE 4.
Letter dated February 7, 1912, from Alvin Langdon Coburn, prominent photographer and member of the Photo-Secession.

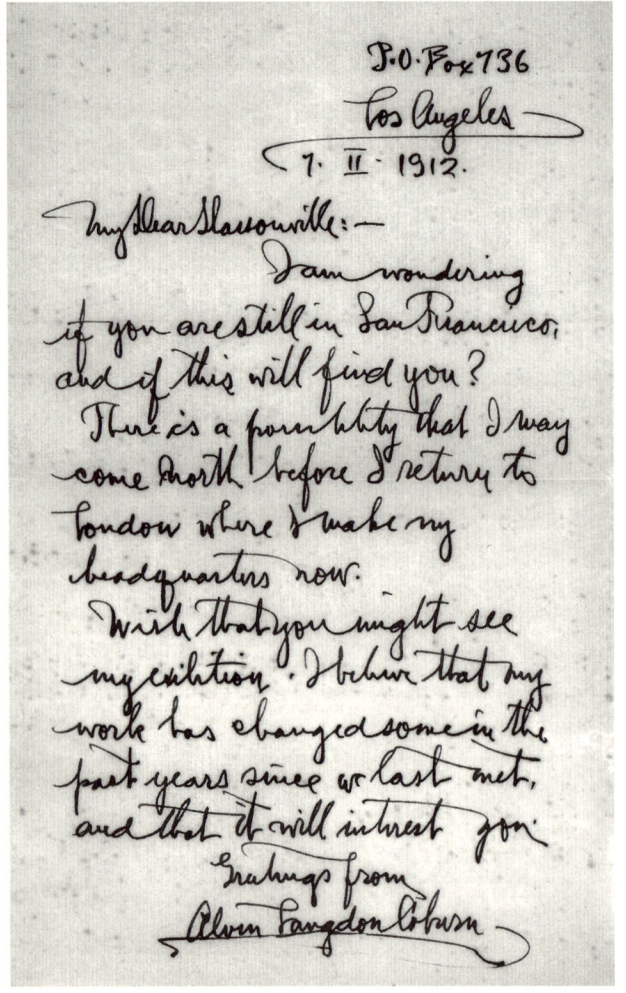

Camera Club. That same month, introduced as an "artist-photographer," he delivered a lecture on the "Application of Artistic Principles to Photography" to members of the club. The next month his article, "The Manipulation of Platinum Paper," appeared in *Camera Craft* (Appendix, p. 93). In this generalized "how-to" on platinum printing, he demonstrated his formidable knowledge and experience: "These formulae have stood the test of my every-day practice for several years."[18]

This was a particularly busy time for Dassonville. He had just completed a photographic excursion to Yosemite in preparation for another solo exhibition of his work at the book store of Paul Elder & Company, 238 Post Street, from October 15th to 31st, 1904. Elder observed that the Dassonville photographs of Yosemite, "show his characteristic strength of composition to a marked degree, and seemingly exceed the limitations of the camera, interpret the height and atmosphere of the valley."[19]

That same year Dassonville also set his sights on the first American Photographic Salon in New York. Out of 9,000 submissions, only about 400 works were retained for exhibition, including Dassonville's photograph entitled, "Portrait," heralded as "a clever study in black and white, [that] will attract attention anywhere."[20] Works by fellow California photographers Oscar Maurer, Adelaide Hanscom, and Laura Adams Armer were also displayed. This exhibit traveled to several major cities across the country, among them Chicago, Portland, and lastly, San Francisco, in April 1905.

In December 1904, Dassonville exhibited as an "active member" in the Second Annual Exhibition of the Guild of Arts and Crafts at the Saint Francis Hotel in downtown San Francisco. The Guild counted as its members painters, ceramicists, leather workers, and sculptors as well as photographers. This organization of self-described craftsmen modeled their ideals upon those spawned by William Morris in England in the nineteenth century. Morris and his followers believed that through the production of beautiful hand-crafted objects, human beings could create an environment in harmony with nature. Like their English counterparts, San Francisco Guild members decried the factory mass-production of "objects of art." Their credo stated: "No mechanical appliance can produce work that has the direct guidance of the individual – his personal touch, judgement and taste." The camera, apparently, did not qualify as a mechanical appliance under these guidelines.

Besides Dassonville, other exhibitors were Adelaide Hanscom, Anne Brigman, Blanche Cummings, Emily Pitchford, and Oscar Maurer. Dassonville's entry was the largest, with seventeen works, priced at $5.00, $10.00 or $15.00. His "Portrait of a Child" was listed as "Sold" in the exhibition, and his photograph "Dome, Yosemite" (Pl. 13) was published in the catalogue.[21]

Membership in the Guild brought Dassonville in close touch with the local art community, among them the painters Xavier Martinez and Maynard Dixon, whom he had photographed as early as 1902 (Pl. 3). The guiding force of the Guild was the artist Lilian W. Tobey, soon to be Dixon's first wife.[22] Another contact was Charles Sedgewick Aiken, editor of the Southern Pacific Company's *Sunset* magazine, who published several of Dassonville's views of coastal Monterey and Carmel in the February 1905 issue.

Exported to the United States, the Arts and Crafts movement flourished in California, where a salubrious climate and magnificent natural geography were combined with a love of nature. Camping in the Sierra Nevada was popular, and John Muir's concept of the "gentle wilderness" was enthusiastically embraced. Artists focused on the landscape. Many of Dassonville's painter friends including Keith, Dixon, Thomas Hill and John Gamble were masters of the landscape, and the photographer himself was dedicated to this subject in his early work. Romantic – if not particularly accurate – notions of the state's Spanish-Mexican past sparked great interest in the California missions and Hispanic culture. These sentiments were incorporated into the Arts and Crafts movement. Architects such as Greene & Greene adopted the design and traditional building materials from *Californio* homes and missions. And the railroads, eager to bring people to California, commissioned artists and writers, including Dassonville, to extol the picturesque quality of the California missions.[23]

Pictorial photography developed in tandem with the Arts and Crafts movement. Both had a passion for the use of fine materials. The variety of photographic papers that were available, both commercial and hand sensitized, and the constant experimentation with complex printing processes as diverse as the photographers who used them, evoked the craftsman's ideals. The popular earth tones favored by the Arts and Crafts movement were the very colors of pictorial photographs, an array of gentle grays and browns. Even the beautiful and intricate mats made to exhibit the photographs reflected this love of fine materials and serene, muted hues.

They were also influenced by a passion for Japanese art with its emphasis on simplicity, pattern and design. Pictorialist photographers flattened space and suppressed detail by using soft focus lenses, reworking the negative, and printing through a diffusing layer of filmy cloth or other material. Not surprisingly, two of the most popular journals of their respective movements, *Camera Craft*, and *The Craftsman*, offered articles on Japanese art. Both also supported and encouraged the populist belief that the creation of beautiful objects or photographs was possible by ordinary people who developed an artistic sensibility.[24]

Exactly how Dassonville, now in his mid twenties, supported himself is unclear. Did he continue to work at one of the photographic supply stores? Was he able to generate sufficient income by portrait commissions, photographs published in periodicals, and the occasional sale but

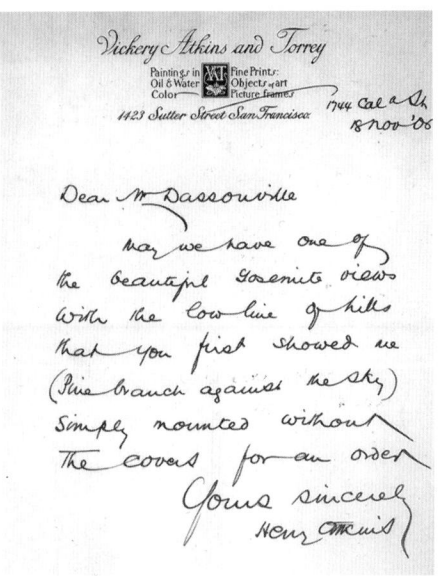

FIGURE 5.
Letter from Henry Vickery of the firm Vickery, Atkins & Torrey, dated November 18, 1906, six months after the April 17, 1906 earthquake and fire in San Francisco, ordering one of Dassonville's recent Yosemite photographs.

FIGURE 6.
The London firm of Willis and Clements was founded by William Willis who invented and patented the platinum printing process in 1873.

uncertain market for his exhibited work? He still resided at the family home at 122 Lyon Street, and this greatly reduced his personal expenses. Major costs centered around his studio, photographic supplies, and travel for his work.

Very slim and nearly 5'11" tall, he smoked a pipe and was partial to Vaponica brand tobacco. He was not yet married. A wry description of Dassonville was provided by Anne Brigman in a letter to Alfred Stieglitz: "Dassonville out here is a queer freaky chap." In similar tone, she sardonically described Arnold Genthe as "very Teutonic, [and] in with rich customers."[25]

On April 18, 1906, Dassonville's studio was wiped out by the devastating San Francisco earthquake and fire. Nothing was saved. The earthquake not only toppled the city, but it created a disruption in the artistic community that would take years to rebuild. Surviving letters from his father to "My dear Eddie" detail the difficulty of coping in the face of great losses in the family business, the overall fiscal uncertainty of the times, and above all, the need to obtain sufficient credit to restart his business. Fortunately, the family home remained intact and continued to provide Dassonville with a base to begin anew.

Although his studio and most if not all of his pre-1906 negatives had been lost, he continued to exhibit his remaining photographs. An April 1907 show at the Hotel del Monte Art Gallery in Monterey was followed in September by an exhibition in the newly re-established club rooms of the California Camera Club. Presumably, these prints had been part of various out-of-San Francisco exhibitions or had survived at his home. Moreover, he was quickly rebuilding his negative collection, as noted by Fayette J. Clute, editor of *Camera Craft*, in his summary article, "Work in the Western States," for *Photograms of the Year 1907*. He wrote "W. E. Dassonville has confined his efforts almost exclusively to landscape work since the fire ... he has secured a wonderfully fine set of Yosemite Valley pictures, and has also exploited other districts in his usual masterful style."[26] (Fig. 5)

The years after the earthquake were marked by a continuation of a now well-established routine, a mixture of assignments and exhibitions. In the summer of 1908 he made a series of masterful portraits of painter William Keith (Pl. 17) who was then about seventy years of age. At Dassonville's suggestion, Keith had moved his studio to the top floor of the Hirsch-Kayser Building at 220 Post Street, directly across from the photographer's studio.

The relationship between the two men blossomed. Since nearby restaurants were destroyed by the earthquake, Dassonville had set up a kitchenette in his studio, and the two men had lunch there several times a week. "Keith enjoyed the fare of honey and bread, or toast, or English muffins; he liked the coziness of the place and above all, the

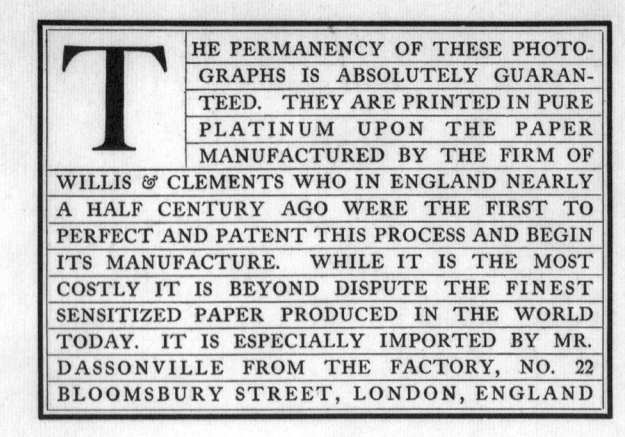

congenial spirit of his friend." In his fondness for Dassonville, Keith also volunteered financial assistance: "If you ever need any money come to me and I'll let you have it." After Keith's death in 1911, Edward N. Harmon, his son-in-law and executor, had Dassonville photograph all the paintings in the painter's estate. This project must have been extensive, for the cost of these services was more than three thousand dollars.[27]

Despite the destruction of his studio, examples of Dassonville's work before 1906 happily have survived. His earliest-known images, taken around 1900, are wintry landscapes of the Sacramento River Valley. One of these, "A November Day" (Pl. 2) was exhibited in the First San Francisco Salon in 1901. Soon he was photographing Yosemite, the High Sierra, the Pacific coast around Monterey, Carmel, and Santa Barbara, and Marin County north of San Francisco, places he often returned to for subject matter in the years before 1915.[28]

Many of his landscape photographs, particularly those made in Yosemite, reveal a sharp-focus naturalism reminiscent of the work of Peter Henry Emerson (Pl. 20). With their precisely delineated silvery tones, these images demonstrate Dassonville's superb craftsmanship and mastery of the platinum process, and perhaps presage Ansel Adams' development of the "zone system" for exposure control. Other landscapes from this first period of Dassonville's work are more classically pictorial in style. Their soft focus supresses details and creates a dreamy, lyrical mood. Frequently the dark shapes of trees are silhouetted against a light-filled sea, sky, or distant hills (Pl. 9). Space is flattened, and Japanese-inspired compositional devices such as the sinuous curve of a stream (Pl. 19), or a shoreline (Pl. 9), or a radically tilted picture plane (Pl. 6), convey a sense of a distance.[29]

Dassonville utilized the platinum process more than any other, but he also worked frequently with gum bichromate. Platinum and gum prints made from the same landscape negative often provided strikingly different effects. For portraits he favored platinum printing, and advertised that he used only papers by Willis & Clement, the first to perfect and patent platinum-based emulsions (Fig. 6). His discovery of a sheer, translucent paper imported from Japan excited him; it produced luminous gum bichromate prints that seemed to emanate light (Pl. 14). In October 1908, a collection of prints on this Japanese tissue destined for an Austrian collector (but now lost), were shown at the galleries of Vickery, Atkins & Torrey, 550 Sutter Street (Fig. 7).[30] The true craftsman, Dassonville continued to experiment with new printing materials over the next twenty years.

During the first decade of the century, Dassonville was commissioned by the Southern Pacific Railroad Company to photograph several of California's Franciscan missions. Surviving correspondence indicates that at Mission Santa Barbara he also did on-site portraits of the priests. One photograph, "At Mission Santa Barbara" (Fig. 8) was published as the frontispiece illustration in the February 1909 issue of *Camera Craft*. In a letter dated July 10, 1908, Father Francis commended the photographer:

I am very happy to see that you had such success in spite of the unfavorable weather which you encountered on the second day you were here. In fact, if I may say it, I think the pictures you took on that day are in every respect equal to any of the others. The one of Father Anthony and myself, with the cloaks on, was taken under very unfavorable conditions and yet is quite a favorite here.[31]

FIGURE 7.
Exhibition announcement, Galleries of Vickery, Atkins & Torrey, 1908.

FIGURE 8.
"At Mission Santa Barbara,"
1908, frontispiece,
Camera Craft, vol 16,
no. 2, February 1909.

Three other examples of Dassonville's mission photographs were included in the book, *The Old Spanish Missions of California*, by Paul Elder.

In April 1909 Dassonville received high praise in Lucy B. Jerome's column, "In the Art World," which appeared each Sunday in the *San Francisco Call*. She noted his recent move into a "newly completed" studio at 251 Post Street. Her comments reflect how faithfully his photographs and exhibition rooms fulfilled the craftsman's ideal:

The walls and ceilings of each of the three rooms were tinted and finished after the artist-photographer's orders, the result being a delightfully harmonious and restful combination of colors, accessories and furnishings .... Beauty in some guise greets the eye on every side. The few prints on the walls are chosen with a view to their proper placing and coloring, and altogether this artistic and delightful interior is a place fitted to contain the unusual photographic work exhibited.[32]

On June 6th she again visited Dassonville and observed:

One of the good things promised for the fall will be an exhibition by W. E. Dassonville, whose remarkable work has brought him prominently before the art loving public. Dassonville's studio ... will be the gathering place for about 100 prints, both landscape and portrait .... The idea of the artist is to have a two tone exhibition. The landscape work will be shown in the studio proper, where the walls are of a prevailing subdued orange hue, while the prints will be as nearly as possible on the same tone, thus making an effect both harmonious and poetic. The same principle will be followed out of the smaller room, where the walls are a light French gray, where the portrait work will be displayed.[33]

An unnamed local artist who was visiting the studio at the same time, remarked upon leaving: "I won't say that your prints look like drawings, but merely that I shall endeavor now to get my drawings to look as much like prints as possible."[34]

Dassonville's portrait business continued to grow and by 1910 boasted customers of significant financial means, many of whom came considerable distances for their sittings. Most of these new clients could easily afford to travel by steamer and to stay in luxury hotels such as the Saint Francis in San Francisco, and the immensely popular Hotel del Monte in Monterey. In September, author Ina Coolbrith wrote to request additional copies of her portrait and thanked Dassonville for a print of William Keith's profile portrait: "I have shown it – proudly – to my friends, to their great admiration, and told them how kind you were." Among the visitors during this same period were naturalist John Burroughs and writer Charles Keeler. Burroughs sat for his portrait, and a copy was later given to Keeler who deemed it "splendid." Burroughs, by contrast, was less enthusiastic: "Makes me look too old, wife says, but all photos do that."[35]

Dassonville had been busy in other ways as well. His new studio and the increased publicity widened his contacts with wealthy San Franciscans. A young socialite who was seriously injured in an automobile accident had visited his studio during her recuperation and on November 5th, they eloped. Dassonville's bride was Miss Gertrude Blanche Perry, the daughter of Dr. and Mrs. E. E. Perry of the wealthy Marin County town of Ross. The ceremony was performed without fanfare and described as a "quiet church wedding." The *San Francisco Chronicle* of Monday, November 7, 1910, headlined the event on page 14: "News of Wedding Startles Society.... Daughter of Wealthy San Franciscan, Wife of Artist-Photographer." The bride's father had objected to the marriage and these objections were dropped "only when the parents were informed by telephone from San Francisco that the marriage was about to take place." The bride had been among the most recent crop of debutantes and "attended many society functions including the Greenway Ball at the Fairmont" Hotel.

> MR. DASSONVILLE *at all times welcomes the opportunity of showing to visitors the collection of photographs, in both landscape and portraiture, permanently on exhibition in the studio.*
>
> 140 Geary Street
> San Francisco

> MR · W · E · DASSONVILLE
> ANNOUNCES THAT HIS STUDIO
> IS NOW PERMANENTLY LOCATED IN
> THE SACHS BUILDING
> 140 GEARY STREET
> SAN FRANCISCO
>
> THESE premises have been designed by Mr. Dassonville and built under his personal supervision. They embody, therefore, all that is essential to the perfection of the modern photographic art.
>
> On the ground of past achievement, Mr. Dassonville feels confident that the perfection of his present Studio will enable him to carry still higher the standards of his work. Visitors are cordially welcome to inspect the photographic prints displayed.

FIGURE 9.
January 16, 1914, card announcing Dassonville's new portrait studio at 140 Geary St., San Francisco.

Comment about the groom was largely limited to the fact that he was a friend of the artist, William Keith, and had "attracted considerable attention by an exhibition and sale in London of art photographs." And finally by the terse but disdainful: "He is not a society man." The couple honeymooned in secrecy.[36]

Details of the Dassonvilles' early married life are sparse. After residing briefly at 1595 Clay Street, the couple moved across the bay to Alameda County while William maintained his studio in San Francisco. He still enjoyed the bohemian status of "artist-photographer," and probably was not warmly welcomed as a true member of the high society circles in which Gertrude had moved as an unmarried young woman. She too, may have found herself less popular with her former crowd.

On February 16, 1912, William's father, wrote to "My

FIGURE 10.
From Dassonville's promotional brochure for Christmas 1914.

AN APPRECIATION

FIGURE 11.
From Dassonville's promotional brochure for Christmas 1914.

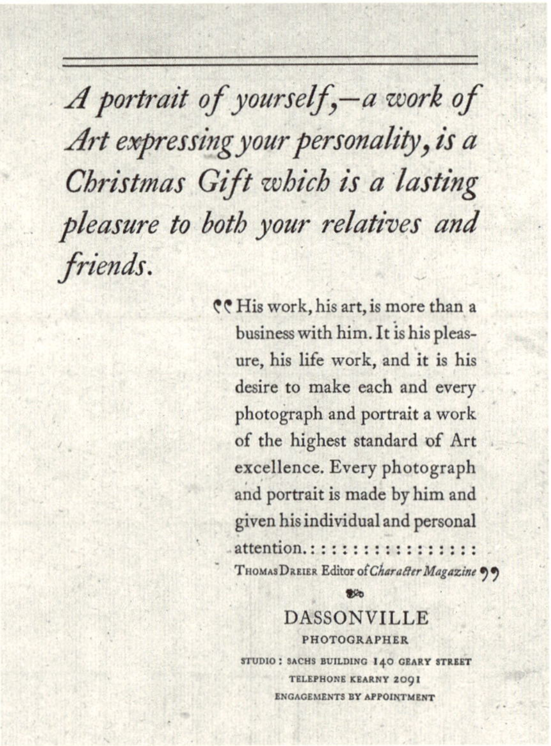
A portrait of yourself,—a work of Art expressing your personality, is a Christmas Gift which is a lasting pleasure to both your relatives and friends.

"His work, his art, is more than a business with him. It is his pleasure, his life work, and it is his desire to make each and every photograph and portrait a work of the highest standard of Art excellence. Every photograph and portrait is made by him and given his individual and personal attention.: : : : : : : : : : : : : : : :
THOMAS DREIER Editor of *Character Magazine*"

DASSONVILLE
PHOTOGRAPHER
STUDIO: SACHS BUILDING 140 GEARY STREET
TELEPHONE KEARNY 2091
ENGAGEMENTS BY APPOINTMENT

dear Ed and Gertrude. I suppose congratulations are in order over the Valentine Gertrude handed Ed. I received the telegram same night, and today Gertrude's letter. I suppose you think that the only baby."[37] The subject of this letter was the couple's daughter Marion, born on Valentine's Day.

Almost exactly two years later, a handsome brochure (Fig. 9) announced the establishment of Dassonville's new studio "now permanently located in the Sachs Building, 140 Geary Street, San Francisco." Noting that it was designed and built under "his personal supervision," he invited the public to view "the collection of photographs, in both landscape and portraiture, permanently on exhibition in the studio."[38] For Christmas 1914, he solicited business with an elegant card (Figs. 10, 11) containing a tipped-in portrait and an endorsement by Thomas Dreier, editor of *Character* magazine:

> *I admire these Dassonville portraits. They express the individual personality. They are real portraits – not mere likenesses – and Master Craftsman that he is, he will make his prints only upon Platinum, which he knows to be permanent. His work, his art, is more than a business with him. It is his pleasure, his life work.*[39]

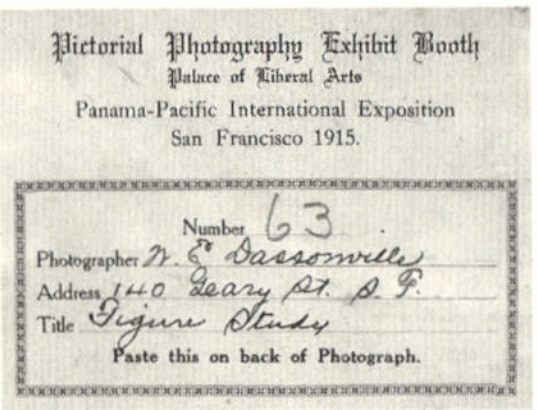
Pictorial Photography Exhibit Booth
Palace of Liberal Arts
Panama-Pacific International Exposition
San Francisco 1915.

Number 63
Photographer W. E. Dassonville
Address 140 Geary St. S. F.
Title Figure Study
Paste this on back of Photograph.

FIGURE 12.
Label for "Figure Study" (Pl. 16) exhibited at the 1915 Panama Pacific International Exposition.

The year 1915 was a hallmark year for San Francisco and California. Now recovered from the effects of the 1906 earthquake, the city hosted the Panama Pacific International Exposition. The grand Beaux Arts exposition buildings stood at the edge of San Francisco Bay atop land-fill completed expressly for this purpose. Photography was exhibited in the Palace of Liberal Arts (it failed to earn a spot in the Palace of Fine Arts despite loud objections from the local photography community). Among the photographs that Dassonville exhibited were "Bell, Mission San Juan Capistrano" (Pl. 8), for which he won an Honorable Mention in the Pictorial section; "Day Dreams" (Pl. 10); and "Figure Study" (Fig. 12 and Pl. 16). Writing in the *American Annual of Photography*, R. H. Danforth reviewed the photographer's contributions:

> *Turning to the Pacific Coast work, there were twelve pieces submitted by W. E. Dassonville of San Francisco which were given much merited praise. These included several beautiful portraits, in which excellence in the handling of the general pose was specially shown. Striking in its simplicity, and in a peculiar yellowish gray tone under the gallery light, was the "Portrait of a Child," which was one of the best things Dassonville had. A beautiful head of John Muir, betraying at once the strength and the gentleness of the naturalist, was hung near it. Carmel, that Mecca of all wise western pictorialists, had been drawn upon by the exhibitor for some good sea-and-land compositions.*[40]

Dassonville's prominence as a portrait photographer and his busy exhibition schedule were matched by the numerous publications in which his work was reproduced in this period. A portrait of William Keith appeared as the frontispiece for Edward Robeson Taylor's *In the Keith Room at the Exposition*, and his late-in-life likeness of John Muir was the frontispiece in the February 1915 issue of *Camera Craft*.[41] Three Muir portraits were also published in a special tribute to the naturalist in the *Sierra Club Bulletin* of January 1916. Promoting tourism in California, Thomas G. Murphy's *Sunset Highways: A Book of Motor Rambles in California* contained twelve of his photographs. Paul Elder's *California the Beautiful* with the photographer's image, "Mount Tamalpais," had the more literary aim of combining "Camera studies by California artists with selections in prose and verse from western writers." Another collaboration so typical of the California artistic community in which Dassonville flourished, was *Yosemite: An Ode*, with poetry by George Sterling (Fig. 13) and five images by the photographer reproduced as photogravures (Pls. 14, 15). On the title page of Dassonville's copy, Sterling inscribed "This ode falls down in spots; but your pictures are *always* good" (Fig. 14).[42]

On October 29th, 1915, Dassonville's second child Donald was born, but he persisted in his preoccupation with work. The dampening effect of World War I undermined his commercial prospects just as family responsibilities were growing. Two children and a recently purchased family home at 2034 Lake Street in San Francisco's Richmond District, added to his financial difficulties. By 1917, his photographs had all but disappeared from exhibitions and publications. In November 1918, he submitted a poem and a now unknown photograph to *Sunset* magazine. In a terse reply, the editor called the poem "a beautiful thing and good use can be made of it," but termed the photograph "most unsatisfactory," words which must have shocked Dassonville.[43]

The war and its need for metals caused a critical shortage of platinum printing papers. Dassonville's work, his art, and his portraiture, depended heavily upon an increasingly scarce product. It was time for adjustments. With a need for a platinum-like substitute and knowledge and skill in chemistry, he began to experiment with the process of coating photographic papers.

He reappeared as an exhibitor and public speaker in the

FIGURE 13.
"George Sterling, Poet", ca. 1905, by William Dassonville.

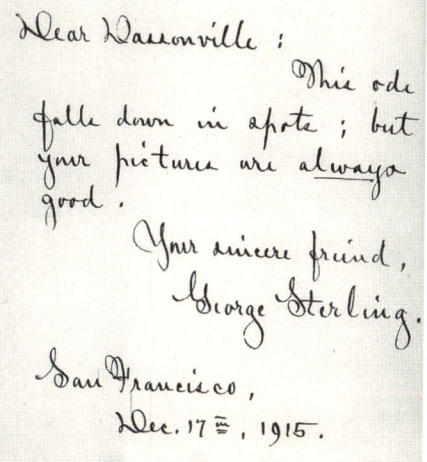

FIGURE 14.
Inscription from George Sterling in Dassonville's copy of Yosemite: An Ode.

AN APPRECIATION   21

early 1920s with decidedly commercial goals. In October 1923, one of his entries at the Second San Francisco-Oakland Salon, a portrait of William Keith printed from an earlier negative, was a silver print on paper he had hand-coated. Henry A. Hussey, who wrote a critique noted that Dassonville's paper "secures wonderful richness and quality," and John Paul Edwards termed this image the "best portrait in this exhibition."[44]

The same month Dassonville spoke at length to a forum held by the Photographers' Association of California on the relative merits of contact printing in comparison to enlargement by projection. He emphasized that while there were good papers for contact printing, this was not true for projection techniques. For enlarging, Dassonville maintained "There are very few papers to select from, and these few are, broadly speaking, alike." Then he got to the crux of the matter:

> Now, I think the thing most needed today – and a subject which I have myself worked on very diligently for the last three years – is really high grade, fine enlarging papers, sensitive enough to use for enlarging … [but not overly sensitive so that the exposure is too short to allow manipulation during the projection process] …. I, myself, working with an open stop, have secured negatives on paper coated by myself that have all the charm, all the softness, all the quality of diffusion in the positive which may be gained by projection.[45]

This was the first time Dassonville spoke publicly of his experimentation and he did not lose the opportunity to promote his soon-to-be-available products. His new papers would have the tonal complexity of platinum with its nearly endless range of grays, but since silver-based, would not need to be contact-printed and also be less expensive.

He had donned yet another hat, that of scientist and entrepreneur. His life was increasingly dominated by an absolute need to understand intimately the *science* of photography. In January 1924 Dassonville began a series of talks to members of the California Camera Club (Appendix, pp. 97–104). The first lecture was on "The Metric System," a very dry topic, he confessed, but in it he stressed "if there is any field in which it can truthfully be said that knowledge is power, it is in the field of photography." In February he spoke on "Photographic Plates and Papers," followed by "The Art of Photography" in March, and "The Business of Photography" in April.[46]

In each case Dassonville's grasp of his subject was assured. The following excerpt from "Photographic Plates and Papers" reveals his dedication to seeking a solution to every technical problem, no matter the effort involved:

> So far as the actual physical paper upon which the emulsion is placed, it has these characteristics. It has color, it has weight and it has texture. That is the base upon which the photographic print has to rest. We print on it; and there we are met by these considerations – the gradation [of tone] that we wish, and also this very important point which is easily overlooked – the depth of the deposit can easily confuse you. If the depth is not very great, and the paper is of a harsh type possessing very little graduation, the print will show up soft. The reason is that with lack of depth you do not get contrast, and when contrast is lacking flatness comes in. I puzzled over that for many weeks when I first came upon it. I got short scale papers with great softness, but I was not getting density – and that was the answer. The character of the emulsion harsh or soft, the physical type of the paper, whether or not the speed suits our purpose constitutes the problem.[47]

His final lecture in the series was on the business side of photography. After surveying consumer trends, he spoke of his own experience in the rapidly shrinking portrait business. He noted, "The day of twelve photographs as an order has gone by, the day of six photographs is here, [and] the day of three photographs to an order is closely advancing."

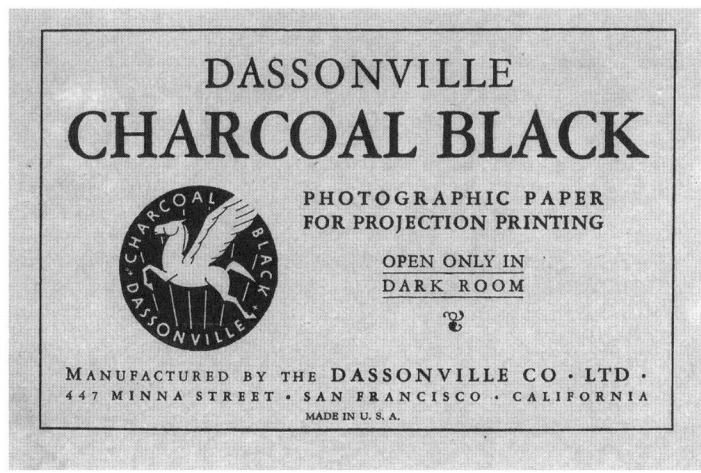

FIGURE 15.
Label from a package of Dassonville Charcoal Black paper.

The trick was to get better pay for fewer prints:

In my own studio the average person for the last two years has been ordering six. Out of every fifty people I photograph I venture to say that thirty-five order six prints; a few order one print and a very few order one, two, three or four dozen. Reorders are, of course, frequent, but the person who orders just one print from me must show me a profit.[48]

By early May, Dassonville was immersed in the business of coating high quality papers with his new silver bromide emulsion. He called his papers "Charcoal Black." Sigismund Blumann, longtime contributor to *Camera Craft* and its editor from 1924 to 1933, quipped, "same individual, same body, same clothes, not the same man." Blumann bought some of the new Charcoal Black paper, tried it, and approved of both the product and the fledgling Dassonville Photographic Paper Company. His essay was published in the May issue of *Camera Craft* and marks the earliest public review of the new Charcoal Black paper. He called Dassonville "a very practical fellow with definite ideas." He found Charcoal Black to be an "exquisitely crisp, substantial, though thin stock with a dead, roughish surface and parchment-like texture ... [also that] the translucence of the paper is one of its elements of beauty."[49]

After years of intense effort and experimentation, Dassonville now burst forth in a frenzy of new business activity. Everything was needed at once, Blumann remarked: "Scientific, delving in paper stock, chemical reactions, thermostatics, profits, markets, demands, and all the details of manufacture and distribution." In July Dassonville sold his portrait studio to concentrate on manufacturing Charcoal Black full time. From his new quarters at 447 Minna Street, he began promoting his product as "not only new in quality & effect but outstandingly artistic," and as "a distinctive paper with all the matte and feeling of platinum." He was also devoting every available dime to his new enterprise (Fig. 15).[50]

Among those who saw him at work in his new undertaking were the writer and photographer Phillip Ennis and Dassonville's son Donald, whose reminiscences were later collected by Janet Lokke. She writes:

Dassonville designed and built all of his own machinery.... His son recalled watching him wander up and down the aisles at Justinian & Caire, "dealers of hardware, assayer's and chemist's materials, wire cloth and grape grower's supplies," at 573–575 Market Street. [He] would lose himself in the place, loading his pockets with gauges and gadgets, while calculating measurements, mechanical flows, temperature key points, and pressure points, [and all the time] drawing plans in his head.[51]

About preparing the Charcoal Black emulsion, Ennis writes:

First step in the intricate process of making photographic paper is brewing the emulsion. In a set of heavy porcelain tanks floating in electrically heated and mechanically agitated water are mixed pure gelatine from the hides of pig, calf and water buffalo from far-off India; bromide of potash with or without a chloride, a fine grade

AN APPRECIATION

FIGURE 16.
Blue Ribbon awarded to Dassonville at Hawaii Territorial Fair, 1926.

nitrate of silver manufactured right here in San Francisco and a shake or two of secret number one. Here the emulsion is "cooked" for ... well, that's secret number two. Then the vats are hoisted by crane and their contents poured into a larger mixer vat which is maintained at proper temperature within a small fraction of one degree. The exact temperature for each emulsion is secret number three.[52]

Lokke details how the paper was coated and hung up to dry:

Constructed of dense, hard maple and stainless steel, the paper-coating machinery was a mass of thermostats and gauges. The paper, in rolls three to four feet wide, was fed into the lead-off, then run through a temperature setting unit where the emulsion was spread on, to a specified thickness. The paper was then carried out in long festoons, held by clips and lifted ceilingward. Just as one loop of paper would drop, the cleet [sic] carrying the rest of the loop would rise to the ceiling. The room became a weaving ribbon of twelve to fourteen foot loops just a few inches apart, running their course like some airborne river.[53]

By controlling the viscosity and temperature of the emulsion, Dassonville attempted to achieve an even distribution, consistent paper sensitivity and tonal response. However the emulsion continued to vary from batch to batch, and he had to test each one and supply test strips and different instructions for timing exposures with each package of paper. In September, *Camera Craft* happily reported that "Charcoal Black has been sold to its capacity and grosses beyond."[54]

Dassonville harnessed his reputation and skill to promote his product. By 1928 photographs on Charcoal Black had been seen in exhibitions five times in San Francisco, in cities across America and Canada such as Dallas, Pittsburgh, Portland, Honolulu, (Fig. 16) Toronto, and Newark, and as far away as Birmingham, England, and Bridge of Allan, Scotland. Two were one-man shows, in San Francisco at Paul Elder's Gallery, and in New Jersey at the Newark Camera Club, where one critic likened his thirty photographs on Charcoal Black to artwork "not ... done since the days when artists ground their own pigments, expressed their own oils and bound their own brushes."[55]

During these years of his greatest commercial success, he made some of his finest photographs. For the first time he embraced urban and industrial subject matter. In a series of views of San Francisco from Telegraph Hill, he silhouetted the dark, flat decorative forms of eucalyptus trees against the city's skyline. This compositional device was one he had favored in his early years, as was the Japanese-inspired motif of depicting distance by horizontal planes piled one on top of another (Pl. 32). He juxtaposed structures such as San Francisco's newest skyscraper, the Russ Building (Pl. 28), against the quainter buildings of the past (Fig. 17).

Dassonville, like many pictorialists at this time, experimented with the subjects, geometries and abstraction of modernism (Pls. 34, 37, 38). From the overlapping and converging cables and superstructures of a ship deck he constructed picture planes of numerous geometric forms (Pls. 33, 35). In his best known photograph of the period, "Beach Grasses," sunlight striking reeds results in an essentially abstract light design (Pl. 24). Nevertheless, like other pictorialists trying out modernist ideas, he adhered loyally to a soft focus vision for which the rich tonal values and textured surfaces of Charcoal Black paper were so perfect.

By 1926 the Dassonville Paper Company had begun to take its place alongside the giant paper makers such as Eastman Kodak, Ansco, Defender, Gevaert and Agfa. Yet all was not well. In May he wrote his father that he was having trouble with one of his suppliers of raw paper stock. "I am going back to the mill [located near Boston] to straighten up the difficulty .... I shall return by New York, Chicago,

Kansas City, etc. and sell in these towns."⁵⁶ The problem was one of consistency:

> He sought out paper makers who would mill for him the texture and weights of paper he desired. That process also proved the most frustrating. With [each] order, Dassonville would give instructions for how the paper was to be made, making sure to include a detailed list of the type and amount of chemicals that were to be left out. He would be adding his own chemicals during the paper-coating process and any change in his directions for the papermaking could and did too often result in the surprise development of a new compound. Invariably some foreman, who did not know what the paper was to be used for and convinced that it would not be strong enough for printing purposes, had made corrections with all good intentions.⁵⁷

Some of his problems could only be put down to bad luck. In one instance he left the water running in his upstairs plant. Below him was Whitman's Chocolates. The overflowing water ruined much of the candy, and Dassonville had to pay for the damage.⁵⁸

Despite setbacks, he succeeded in creating seven grades of photographic paper varying in texture, color and weight. A promotional pamphlet describes them:

> Grade B: Pure white in tone, with artists' true sketching surface .... Medium weight.
> Grade C: A delightful laid paper (lightly ribbed) .... Clear ivory tone.
> Grade D: An exquisite, very rough paper .... Purest white stock.
> Grade E: A pure ivory tone ... pleasing and unusual warmth.
> Grade F: Remarkably translucent [the thinnest stock]. Ideal for enlarged paper negatives; for straight projection prints ... and for printing through the back to gain charming pictorial grain effects.⁵⁹

Curiously, Dassonville never applied for a patent for Charcoal Black. His son Donald believes his father was attempting to keep the formula secret, but it is possible that his difficulty in standardizing the emulsion kept him from seeking a patent.

IN THE mid-1920s, a lanky young pianist-turning-photographer named Ansel Adams met Dassonville at a Camera Club meeting. "Dassonville, he learned, was a neighbor," Nancy Newhall writes. "Dropping in to see him now and then, Ansel absorbed the idea that photography could be an art."⁶⁰ Adams remembered the older photographer from these

FIGURE 17.
"San Francisco," ca. 1927
by William Dassonville.

AN APPRECIATION 25

FIGURE 18.
Advertisement for Dassonville Charcoal Black, with the photographer's portrait of William Keith.

years as "very kind to me" and generous with technical information unlike other photographers who "just hated to give away secrets."[61] He used Charcoal Black to print many of his early photographs, including an image of Mount Robson he made in 1928 on a Sierra Club trip to Jasper National Park, Canada. He printed this image 15 x 11 inches and made a gift of this large photograph to Dassonville, writing on the overmat:

To my Friend W. E. Dassonville – I want you to have this print as an expression of my appreciation – As you see, I have been able to achieve results with a most difficult subject, in a manner that I know could not be gotten with any other photographic paper.[62]

In 1929 when working on his book, *Taos Pueblo*, Adams commissioned Dassonville to prepare the paper. After the specially ordered, rag-base paper had arrived from a New England mill, Dassonville delivered half the paper to the printers for the text pages and coated the other half with his rich silver-bromide Charcoal Black emulsion. The usual practice of adding starch to the paper to achieve a matte surface was abandoned so that Adams would have a paper "as brilliant as I could get."[63] *Taos Pueblo* was published in 1930 with twelve original photographs printed on a Dassonville paper with a lustrous surface.

During the summer of that year, Adams met Paul Strand in New Mexico. Strand's sharply focused 4 x 5 inch negatives of Taos (Strand had no prints to show him) provided the catalyst which finally propelled Adams to leave behind his quasi-pictorial style for a sharper, more detailed vision.[64] Adams, along with Edward Weston, Imogen Cunningham, Willard Van Dyke, Sonya Noskowiak, and several other photographers who believed in what has come to be called "straight photography," banded together to form Group f/64 in 1932. An exhibition of Group f/64 at the de Young Memorial Museum in San Francisco followed that same year. Adams recalled that "The Group f/64 upset Dassonville very much ... the idea that we would have thought the photographic art possible with this glossy, shiny paper. I think it broke his heart."[65]

Nonetheless, Charcoal Black continued to have a strong market into the 1930s; even Ansel Adams used it through about 1933.[66] Two factors eventually undermined the business: the Depression and photographers' growing rejection of pictorial style and materials. Dassonville tried to counteract a precipitous decline in sales with advertisements in camera magazines, promotional lectures, and new products, including a line of developers. An advertisement in the January 1933 issue of *American Photography* announced the introduction of four new grades of the paper. A 1934 advertisement "The Miniature Camera and Charcoal Black ... an excellent team for the making of superlative projection prints" attempted to attract users of the Leica and other newly popular miniature cameras. In 1935 the photographer resorted to sponsoring "The Dassonville Competition." The entrants, of course, were to utilize Charcoal Black in producing their prints; the winners received packages of the product. Finally, the Depression forced Dassonville to reduce his prices and to offer a special introductory package: "18 sheets, 8x10, six of ea. grade," for $1.65 (Fig. 18). His regular prices were tagged as follows, per dozen sheets: 5x7, 65 cents; 8x10, $1.50; and 11x14, $2.95.[67] Eventually he could no longer afford to pay his employees and he let most of them go.

Despite hard times, Dassonville continued to exhibit regularly to favorable reviews, and his photographs appeared in a number of local publications. On April 1, 1934, the San Francisco Chronicle promoted an upcoming speaking engagement in these words: "This beautiful camera study of several silver birch is the work of W. E. Dassonville, internationally known pictorialist, who will speak before the California Camera Club Tuesday evening at 8 o'clock in their club rooms, and will explain the most successful methods of making prints like the one above." In like manner, the Washington, DC Sunday Star reviewed Dassonville's 1933 one-person retrospective at the United States National Museum in the Smithsonian Institution:

FIGURE 19. *"Don Oliver Photographing in the Sierra Nevada,"* ca. 1939, Dassonville's last published photograph in *Camera Craft, appearing as the frontispiece in Vol. 46, No. 11, November, 1939.*

They are of exceptional artistic interest …. Not only does he seem to understand the importance of good composition, but also the value of light and shade, and of atmospheric effect. His prints of the Monterey cypresses are exceptionally fine – trees standing out with character and definiteness, sufficiently but not too greatly defined, their spirit as well as their form interpreted. In quite a different manner Mr. Dassonville transcribes pictures of the dunes. Realizing that here there is no emphasis, he depends upon line and rhythm, delicacy of tone, to give adequate expression. From plate to plate one sees a complete change of mood and yet withal a complete mastery of medium.[68]

During the 1930s, Dassonville returned to photographing his first love the landscape (Pls. 42, 44). He concentrated on the Sierra Nevada (Fig. 19), the Owens Valley, and the White Mountains on the California-Nevada border, site of the bristle cone pine, the world's oldest living trees. By this time Dassonville had adopted a largely "sharp focus" approach (although he continued to print on Charcoal Black). The influence of Ansel Adams and other members of Group f/64 is undeniable. Certainly he would not have failed to see their work reproduced in *Camera Craft* and other journals of those years. In particular, his close-up views of natural forms such as rocks and tree trunks reflect their influence, exhibiting an interest in surface texture and detail not previously seen in his work (Pls. 43, 45). Near the end of the decade, he photographed the World's Fair at Treasure Island (Fig. 20) and the Golden Gate Bridge (Pl. 47).

AN APPRECIATION

FIGURE 20.
"William Dassonville Photographing at the Golden Gate International Exhibition, Treasure Island, San Francisco" by photographer Franklin J. Enos, ca. 1939–1940.

MEANWHILE, his personal life was crumbling. He separated from Gertrude in 1936 and was divorced the following year. In a recent interview his son Donald explained that "The divorce was primarily due to my sister and her discontent over the modest income and lifestyle of our family. She spent much time with a girl friend from a very wealthy family. Marion brought home her dissatisfaction and this discontent spread to our mother as well." Not only had Dassonville devoured great chunks of the family income – Donald remembers that the family even had difficulty paying the grocery bills – but he was gone day and night, trying to keep the business alive. Following the divorce, Gertrude and Marion moved to an apartment on Powell Street and received financial support from Gertrude's wealthy family. Eventually they moved to New York City and severed their ties with William and Donald.[69]

After his divorce, Dassonville maintained his hectic schedule nursing the failing paper business. Unfortunately, the wonderful 1940 review by Philip L. Ennis in the *San Francisco Chronicle*, "San Francisco Firm Makes the Famous Charcoal Black" (quoted previously in this essay) came too late. At age sixty-two, Dassonville had taken the company as far as he could, and in 1941 the business – its formulas and its name – were sold.[70]

But if he believed his involvement in his former company was over, he was mistaken. The new owner soon reported difficulty in producing Charcoal Black; buyers of the product complained that their prints were streaked. His reputation and integrity at risk, Dassonville went east and spent a year in a futile attempt to solve the problems, until an offhand comment by a company employee revealed the building's previous use as a chemical plant. "The fumes and contaminants had hung unnoticed in the air, and gathered in every corner and sill throughout the building. Dassonville took enough chemicals and equipment and processed his emulsion, coated his paper and developed a few sheets in the dark of his hotel room – no streaks."[71]

Although the difficulties were overcome, the new owners apparently did not market Charcoal Black again until 1944. An announcement in April 1944, in *The Professional Photographer*, indicated that Dassonville Charcoal Black, at 205 East 42nd Street, New York City, had returned to the market. Advertisements for the paper appeared in photography magazines until the late 1940s. The last one was found in *The Camera* in January 1948; after that, Charcoal Black disappeared.

Eager to stay active, Dassonville found work as a medical photographer at Stanford University's hospital in San Francisco. He continued to work in his darkroom at home and "turned, too, to gardening, seeking to rekindle the joy of producing beautiful things, planting begonias, primrose, fuschias, laying down paths and building redwood walks, flooding the yard with a profusion of dahlias."[72]

San Francisco photographer Phiz Mezey, whose first job after college was as Dassonville's assistant at the hospital in 1948, remembered him as a perfectionist, whose darkroom and laboratory were "immaculate." She was impressed by his skills and remarked that he was still working past the mandatory retirement age of sixty-five. He did not permit her to make test strips before printing, she recalled. He insisted that she "look at the negative, analyze it, and print it."[73]

Dassonville died of a cerebral hemorrhage in San Francisco on July 15, 1957, at the age of seventy-eight, a figure in the history of photography perhaps remembered for his Charcoal Black, but largely forgotten for his photographs. Death notices appeared in the San Francisco newspapers, but there was no obituary or praise by his remaining peers.

Among William Edward Dassonville's surviving papers was found a worn scrap with a horoscope drawn upon it. In the center he wrote his name, and below it penned seven lines with a total of forty-four words. With this, Dassonville may well have written the epitaph for his own remarkable life:

Good conscience, Great sensitiveness.
Superior nature. Great obstacles in life.
Hard struggles. Voyages many, but unprofitable.
Some gain therein, however if Jupiter be in
good aspect. Honors through hard work and
a steady adherence to ones path in life.
Strong imagination. Dreamy & poetical nature.[74]

Notes

1. Ansel Adams, *Examples: The Making of Forty Photographs*, p. 92.
2. Dassonville assembled a small collection of paintings by California artists, among them William Keith, John Gamble, Granville Redmond, Guiseppe Cadanaso and Mary Curtis Richardson. He corresponded with prominent Americans including John Burroughs, Ina Coolbrith, Frederic Goudy, and Alvin Langdon Coburn.
3. Susan Herzig and Paul M. Hertzmann, "Notes on William Dassonville from Conversations with Donald Dassonville, October 24-26, 1997"; letters to Susan and Paul from Donald, August 31, 1997 and October 27, 1998.

    Other family information is derived from a brief unpublished essay by Donald Dassonville: "William E. Dassonville, Photographic Artist," (May 31, 1985). Inasmuch as each of these resources duplicate and/or supplement each other, they are hereafter collectively cited as Donald's Notes.

    Two short unpublished essays by Janet Lokke entitled "W. E. Dassonville – The Photographer as Artist" (ca. 1981) (refererred to as "Photographer as Artist"/Dassonville Papers) and "Dassonville" (1981) (referred to as "Dassonville"/ Dassonville Papers) were based partly on Donald's recollections and are in his possession. All additional surviving Dassonville correspondence and ephemera are hereafter cited as Dassonville Papers.
4. *Overland Monthly*, a fine innovative San Francisco literary magazine founded in 1868, published poetry, short fiction and non-fiction. Many nationally known writers contributed to its pages, including Bret Harte (its first editor), Ambrose Bierce, Jack London, and John Muir. It existed well into the twentieth century.
5. W. E. Dassonville, "Individuality in Photography," *Overland Monthly*, October 1902, pp. 340-345.
6. Donald's Notes.
7. *Camera Craft*, May 1900, p. 32.
8. Ibid., December 1900, p. 160.
9. H. D'Arcy Power, a San Francisco physician, was born in Hamburg Germany in 1857. He attended Charing Cross Medical School in London and graduated from the Royal College of Physicians after earning his doctoral degree in 1883. He moved to Oregon in 1892 and then to California. Power was an amateur photographer active in the California Camera Club, and a tireless and prolific writer on all aspects of photography. Anne Brigman considered him a close friend and "an excellent technician, but not much of a pictorialist." It is likely that Power and Dassonville shared a common interest in the technical side of photography.
10. *Camera Craft*, February 1901, p. 295.
11. Ibid., May 1901, p. 21.
12. "The Second San Francisco Photographic Salon, Its Strong and Weak Points with a Criticism of Its Striking Features," *Camera Craft*, January 1902, p. 125.
13. Helen L. Davie, "The Los Angeles Exhibition, Its History and Success and Those Responsible for It," *Camera Craft*, June 1902, p. 47.

    Camera Craft, June 1902, p. 100.

    Paul Elder, 1872-1948, was a San Francisco bookseller, publisher and editor. His bookshop, founded in 1898, exhibited work by local artists and craftspersons, and he was one of the first San Franciscans to exhibit "artistic" photography. He published under his own name and under the imprint Tomoye Press. His books are still collected for their typographical beauty.
14. "Individuality," p. 343.
15. Ibid.
16. Arnold Genthe, "The Third San Francisco Salon," *Camera Craft*, November 1903, pp. 212-213.
17. Correspondence, Alvin Langdon Coburn to W. E. Dassonville, February 1, 1912, Dassonville Papers. The wedding invitation was postmarked October 26, 1912; this postdated the wedding which took place on the 11th of October.
18. *Camera Craft*, September 1904, p. 174.
    W. E. Dassonville, "The Manipulation of Platinum Paper," *Camera Craft*, October 1904, pp. 187-190.
19. Paul Elder quoted in Lokke, "Dassonville," p. 3, Dassonville Papers.
20. Jeanne E. Bennett, "First American Salon," *Camera Craft*, January 1905, p. 29.
21. *Catalogue: Second Annual Exhibition of the Guild of Arts and Crafts*, San Francisco, December 1904.

22. Xavier Martinez, 1869–1943, was a Mexican-born tonalist painter, etcher and lithographer, and a colorful, well-liked bohemian figure in the San Francisco art world. He taught at the California College of Arts and Crafts from 1909 until 1942.
    Another portrait of Dixon by Dassonville from the same sitting appeared in *Camera Craft*, October 1902.
    Lilian West Tobey, ca. 1880–c.1925, was a painter and craftsperson, and president of the Arts and Crafts Guild of San Francisco in 1904.
23. Details on the Arts and Crafts movement in California are drawn primarily from Timothy J. Andersen, Eudorah M. Moore, and Robert W. Winter, editors, *California Design 1910*.
24. Christian Peterson, "American Arts and Crafts: The Photograph Beautiful 1895–1915," *History of Photography* 16, No. 33, autumn 1992, pp. 189–232.
25. Correspondence, Anne W. Brigman to Alfred Stieglitz, February 19, 1907; copy in the Archives of California Art, The Oakland Museum.
26. Fayette J. Clute, "Work in the Western States," *Photograms of the Year* 1907, p. 96.
27. Details of Keith's life and his friendship with Dassonville are based on Brother Cornelius' book, *Keith: Old Master of California*.
28. In 1901 Dassonville took his only trip to Europe, including Paris, Belgium and the Netherlands. He exhibited prints from this trip in the salons. All these prints have been lost; they are known only from references and illustrations in the literature.
29. Dassonville's library included books on Japan by Lafcadio Hearn. Hearn was a journalist who moved from the U.S. to Japan; his chief works are written for English-speaking people, and interpret Japanese culture.
30. Vickery, Atkins & Torrey, one of the earliest and most important galleries for paintings, prints, sculpture, photography, Chinese porcelains and other art objects, was established by W. K. Vickery in the 1880s. With added partners in the 1890s, Henry Atkins and Frederick Torrey, it flourished well into the twentieth century, going out of business during the depression in 1933.
31. Correspondence, Father Francis to W. E. Dassonville, July 10, 1908, Dassonville Papers.
32. Lucy B. Jerome, "In the Art World," *San Francisco Call*, April 4, 1909.
33. Ibid., June 6, 1909, p. 31.
34. Ibid.
35. Correspondence, Ina Coolbrith to W. E. Dassonville, September 22, 1910, Dassonville Papers.
    Correspondence, John Burroughs to W. E. Dassonville, October 12, [1909], Dassonville Papers.
36. "News of Wedding Startles Society," *San Francisco Chronicle*, November 7, 1910.
37. Dassonville Papers.
38. Dassonville Papers. The undated announcement was titled "W. E. Dassonville/ Photographic Portraits in Platinum and in Color."
39. Dassonville Papers.
40. Roy Harrison Danforth, "Photography at the Exposition," *American Annual of Photography*, 1916, p. 288.
41. Dassonville Papers. This item is autographed, "This copy of a tribute to a great artist is presented to W. E. Dassonville, no less an artist in photography, by his friend, Edward Robeson Taylor, November 14, 1915."
42. George Sterling, *Yosemite: An Ode*: Dassonville Papers. Sterling was a San Francisco poet and prominent figure in the city's literary community. Between 1902 and 1926 he published eleven volumes of poetry. He edited all of Jack London's books (they were close friends). Sterling committed suicide in 1926 on the eve of a Bohemian Club dinner honoring H. K. Mencken, which he was scheduled to attend.
43. Correspondence, Charles K. Reid to W. E. Dassonville, November 5, 1918, Dassonville Papers.
44. Henry A. Hussey, "The San Francisco-Oakland Salon 1923," *Camera Craft*, October 1923, p. 460.
    John Paul Edwards, "The San Francisco-Oakland Salon," *Photo Era*, December 1923, p. 315.
45. "For the Professional," *Camera Craft*, November 1923, pp. 542–543. Dassonville was followed at the podium by John Paul Edwards.

46. W. E. Dassonville, "The Metric System," *Camera Craft*, February 1924, pp. 94–96; "Photographic Plates and Papers," *Camera Craft*, March 1924, pp. 141–143.
    "The Art of Photography," *Camera Craft*, April 1924, pp. 194–195; "The Business of Photography," *Camera Craft*, May 1924, pp. 242–244.
47. "Plates and Papers," p. 142.
48. "The Business Side," p. 242.
49. A paper produced by Eastman Kodak and soon to be sold to Defender, called Carbon Black, was already on the market.
    Sigismund Blumann, "Charcoal Black: A New and Different Photographic Paper," *Camera Craft*, May 1924, pp. 217–220.
50. Ibid., p. 217.
    "Gives Up Studio," *Camera Craft*, July 1924, p. 356. Dassonville sold his studio to L. R. Carlton of the La Fayette Studio. An example of his new Charcoal Black notice appears in the advertising section of *Camera Craft*, October 1924.
51. Lokke, "Dassonville," p. 4, Dassonville Papers.
52. Philip L. Ennis, "Photography: San Francisco Firm Makes the Famous Charcoal Black," *San Francisco Chronicle*, November 10, 1940.
53. Lokke, "Dassonville," p. 4, Dassonville Papers.
54. "Dassonville Paper Company," *Camera Craft*, September 1924, p. 459.
55. "The Newark Camera Club," *Camera Craft*, April 1925, p. 208.
56. Correspondence, W. E. Dassonville to Frederick Dassonville, May 1, 1926, Dassonville Papers.
57. Lokke, "The Photographer as Artist," Dassonville Papers, unpaginated.
58. Donald's Notes.
59. Dassonville Papers, unpaginated.
60. Nancy Newhall, *Ansel Adams: The Eloquent Light*, Vol. 1, p. 31.
61. Ansel Adams, "Conversations with Ansel Adams," an oral history conducted 1972, 1974, 1975 by Ruth Teiser and Catherine Harroun, Regional Oral History Office, The Bancroft Library, University of California, 1978, pp. 8, 51.
62. This photograph as well as Dassonville's personal copy of Adams' *Taos Pueblo* were sold by the photographer's son in the 1970s, to John Howell Books, then a prominent San Francisco antiquarian bookstore. They are currently in private collections.
63. Ansel Adams, "Conversations with Ansel Adams," p. 128.
64. Ansel Adams, *An Autobiography*, pp. 109–110.
65. Ansel Adams quoted in Lokke, "The Photographer as Artist," Dassonville Papers, unpaginated.
66. Ansel Adams, *An Autobiography*, p. 90.
67. *The Camera*, October 1931, p. 19. This was the first Dassonville advertisement in this magazine.
68. Leila Mechlin, "Notes of Art and Artists," *Sunday Star*, Washington, DC, December 17, 1933, p. 12.
69. Donald's Notes.
70. The last announcement in *Camera Craft* for Charcoal Black from Dassonville's Minna Street address appeared in the April 1941 issue, page 220. Dassonville's son understood that the buyer of the business was named Campbell. This has not been verified.
71. Lokke, "The Photographer as Artist," Dassonville Papers, unpaginated.
72. Ibid.
73. Interview with Phiz Mezey by Susan Herzig and Paul Hertzmann, November 1, 1998.
74. Dassonville Papers.

FIGURE 21.
Printed postcard announcement of a lecture by P. Douglas Anderson, January 20, 1940, using photographs by Dassonville.

M. H. DE YOUNG MEMORIAL MUSEUM
Golden Gate Park, San Francisco, California

The next
PHOTOGRAPHIC CHAT
by
P. DOUGLAS ANDERSON, F. R. P. S.
Lecturer in Photography, University of California Extension Division,
will be given on the afternoon of Saturday, Jan. 20th at 3:00 o'clock.
For illustration, Mr. Anderson will use prints by Mr. W. E. Dassonville
YOU AND YOUR FRIENDS ARE CORDIALLY INVITED

Plates

PLATE 1.
Freesia.
*Platinum print,
ca. 1900. Courtesy of
Paul M. Hertzmann, Inc.*

PLATE 2.
A November Day.
Gum bichromate print, ca. 1900. Courtesy of Michael G. & Jane Wilson.

PLATE 3.
Maynard Dixon,
Painter.
Platinum print, 1901.
Courtesy of Dixon Family
Collection.

[36

PLATE 4.
Portrait of
Alvin Langdon Coburn.
*Platinum print,
ca. 1904. Courtesy of
George Eastman House.*

PLATE 5. Carmel Dunes. *Platinum print, ca. 1905. Courtesy of the Dassonville Trust.*

PLATE 6.
Monterey Coast.
*Platinum print,
ca. 1905. Courtesy of
the Dassonville Trust.*

PLATE 7. Courtyard, Mission San Luis Rey de Francia. *Gum bichromate print, ca. 1905. Courtesy of the Dassonville Trust.*

PLATE 8.
Bell, Mission
San Juan Capistrano.
*Gum bichromate print,
ca. 1905. Courtesy of
the Dassonville Trust.*

PLATE 9.
Carmel Point.
Gum bichromate print, ca. 1905. Courtesy of the Dassonville Trust.

PLATE 10. Day Dreams. *Platinum print, ca. 1910. Courtesy of the Dassonville Trust.*

PLATE 11. North Dome from Yosemite Valley. *Platinum print, ca. 1906. Courtesy of Merrily & Tony Page, Page Imageworks.*

Plate 12. Yosemite Valley. *Platinum print, ca. 1906. Courtesy of Nevada Museum of Art, Reno, Nevada, Permanent Collection, Cutts Bequest Purchase.*

PLATE 13. Dome, Yosemite. *Platinum print, ca. 1904. Courtesy of Richard D. & Susan B. Moore.*

PLATE 14.
Twilight, Yosemite
Valley. *Gum bichromate print, ca. 1907. Courtesy of Barry & Gretchen Singer.*

PLATE 15.
Morning, Half-Dome.
Platinum print, 1907.
Courtesy of A. J.
& Diane Kallet.

PLATE 16.
Figure Study.
*Platinum print,
ca. 1906.
Courtesy of Michael G.
& Jane Wilson.*

PLATE 17.
Portrait of William
Keith, Painter.
*Gum bichromate print,
ca. 1908. Courtesy of
the Dassonville Trust.*

PLATE 18. Mount Tamalpais, Marin County. *Platinum print, ca. 1905. Courtesy of the Dassonville Trust.*

PLATE 19. Mount Tamalpais, Marin County. *Platinum print, ca. 1905. Courtesy of Michael G. & Jane Wilson.*

PLATE 20. Pond and Reeds. *Platinum print, ca. 1910. Courtesy of Michael G. & Jane Wilson.*

Plate 21. Oak Trees, del Monte Forest. *Platinum print, ca. 1905. Courtesy of Kathy & Ron Perisho.*

PLATE 22. Farmhouse, Marin County. *Platinum print, ca. 1910. Courtesy of Merrily & Tony Page, Page Imageworks.*

PLATE 23.
Palm Trees,
Santa Barbara.
Platinum print, ca. 1910.
Courtesy of Michael G.
& Jane Wilson.

PLATE 24. *Grasses. Silver print on Charcoal Black paper, ca. 1925. Courtesy of Peter & Nancy Pool.*

PLATE 25. The Great Highway, San Francisco. *Silver print on Charcoal Black paper, ca. 1925. Courtesy of Michael G. & Jane Wilson.*

[58

PLATE 26. The Great Beach, San Francisco. *Silver print on Charcoal Black paper, ca. 1925. Courtesy of Michael G. & Jane Wilson.*

PLATE 27. San Francisco Waterfront. *Silver print on Charcoal Black paper, ca. 1925. Courtesy of private collection.*

PLATE 28.
The Russ Building,
San Francisco.
*Silver print on Charcoal
Black paper, ca. 1925.
Courtesy of private
collection.*

PLATE 29.
Study in Black
and White, II.
*Silver print on Charcoal
Black paper, ca. 1920.
Courtesy of Michael G.
& Jane Wilson.*

PLATE 30. Dunes. *Silver print on Charcoal Black paper, ca. 1925. Courtesy of Michael G. & Jane Wilson.*

PLATE 31. View of Alcatraz Island from Telegraph Hill, San Francisco. *Silver print on Charcoal Black paper, ca. 1925. Courtesy of the Dassonville Trust.*

PLATE 32. Trees, San Francisco, Russ Building under Construction. *Silver print on Charcoal Black paper, ca. 1925.* Courtesy of Michael S. Whalen, Pasadena, California.

PLATE 33. Ship Deck I. *Silver print on Charcoal Black paper, ca. 1925. Courtesy of Paul M. Hertzmann, Inc.*

PLATE 34.
Oil Refinery,
Richmond, California.
Silver print on Charcoal
Black paper, ca. 1925.
Courtesy of Michael G.
& Jane Wilson.

PLATE 35. Ship Deck II. *Silver print on Charcoal Black paper, ca. 1925. Courtesy of Hallmark Photographic Collection, Hallmark Cards Inc., Kansas City, Missouri.*

PLATE 36. Boat Rail and Reflections. *Silver print on Charcoal Black paper, ca. 1925. Courtesy of private collection.*

PLATE 37.
Standard Oil Tank.
Silver print on Charcoal Black paper, ca. 1925. Courtesy of Michael G. & Jane Wilson.

PLATE 38.
The Condensing Tower.
*Silver print on Charcoal Black paper, ca. 1925.
Courtesy of Austin Lamont.*

PLATE 39. Surf and Rocks. *Silver print on Charcoal Black paper, ca. 1925. Courtesy of the Dassonville Trust.*

PLATE 40. Fishing Boats. *Silver print on Charcoal Black paper, ca. 1925. Courtesy of Richard & Strawn Rosenthal.*

PLATE 41.
Floating Logs in Harbor.
Silver print on Charcoal Black paper, ca. 1925. Courtesy of Michael G. & Jane Wilson.

PLATE 42. Owens Valley. *Silver print on Charcoal Black paper, 1930s. Courtesy of the Dassonville Trust.*

PLATE 43. Gnarled Tree, High Sierra. *Silver print on Charcoal Black paper, 1930s. Courtesy of Kathy & Ron Perisho.*

PLATE 44. California Landscape. *Silver print on Charcoal Black paper, ca. 1925. Courtesy of Barry & Gretchen Singer.*

PLATE 45. Gnarled Tree and Granite Face, High Sierra. *Silver print on Charcoal Black paper, 1930s. Courtesy of the Dassonville Trust.*

PLATE 46. Sky, Owens Valley. *Silver print on Charcoal Black paper, 1930s. Courtesy of the Dassonville Trust.*

PLATE 47. Bridge Approach. *Silver print on Charcoal Black paper, ca. 1937. Courtesy of Merrily & Tony Page, Page Imageworks.*

Appendices

Dassonville: Exhibition History

Note: Descriptive titles not written by Dassonville are in parentheses. The existence of catalogues, numbers of photographs exhibited, and titles of photographs are indicated, if known.

1900 ALAMEDA, CALIFORNIA
Alameda Camera Club, April 7.
"A number of platinotypes" exhibited, according to *Camera Craft*, Vol. 1, No. 1, May 1900.

SAN FRANCISCO, CALIFORNIA
Lassen and Bien Opticians, December.
Group exhibition with L. Adams, Piatt, Coombs, Maurer and Street.

1901 SAN FRANCISCO, CALIFORNIA
First San Francisco Photographic Salon, January. Catalogue.
Homeward Paths
Roadside Shadows
A November Day
Sand Dunes
Twilight on the Bay
The Hay Barge
Evening Mists
Early Morning
The Winter World
Morning Lights (illustrated)
Twilight

SAN FRANCISCO, CALIFORNIA
California Club Exhibition of Industrial Arts, Mechanic's Pavilion, April 17–30.

1902 SAN FRANCISCO, CALIFORNIA
Second San Francisco Photographic Salon, California Camera Club and San Francisco Art Association, Mark Hopkins Institute of Art, January 9–23. Catalogue.
Portrait of Mr. H. J. Breuer
Early Morning
A Dutch Fishing Boat
A Landscape
A Bit of Rotterdam
Along the Canal, Holland
A Study
Portrait of Mr. Chas. Dickman
Study of a Nude (illustrated)
Portrait of Mr. C. P. Neilson
Portrait of Miss Boyle
Portrait of Mrs. C. Roundy
Study of a Head
Portrait of Master Roberts

OAKLAND, CALIFORNIA
Second Annual Exhibition of Fine Art, Starr King Fraternity, Maple Hall, February 26–29.
In the Strange Glimmer and Glamor of a Dream

LOS ANGELES, CALIFORNIA
First Los Angeles Photographic Salon at the Los Angeles Camera Club, May 1–10. Catalogue.
Twilight on the Road
Evening

SAN FRANCISCO, CALIFORNIA
Paul Elder and Company, May 22–June 9.
First one-man show.

1903 SAN FRANCISCO, CALIFORNIA
Third San Francisco Photographic Salon at the Mark Hopkins Institute of Art, October 8–24. Catalogue.
Twilight – Holland
Sand Dunes
Boulogne-sur-Mer
Margaret
A Dutch Canal

1904 FOOCHOW, CHINA
Foochow Third Annual Exhibition, May–June.
Awarded first prize for Portraiture; honorable mention for other classes.

SAN FRANCISCO, CALIFORNIA
Photographs of Yosemite Valley, California, Paul Elder and Company, October 15–31.
First one-man exhibition.

NEW YORK, NEW YORK
First American Salon in New York at the Clausen Galleries, 381 Fifth Avenue, under the auspices of the Metropolitan Camera Club of New York and the Salon Club of America, December 5–17. Catalogue.
- *Rotterdam*
- *Mistress A*
- *Portrait*

SAN FRANCISCO, CALIFORNIA
Second Annual Exhibition of the Guild of Arts and Crafts, Red Room, Hotel St. Francis, December. Catalogue.
- *The Dome, Yosemite* (illustrated)
- *Portrait of a Child*
- *Beach at Carmel*
- *Sand Dunes*
- *Sunset*
- *Point Lobos*
- *Point Lobos, a Design*
- *A Pine Branch*
- *Carmel Mission*
- *Cypress Trees*
- *Cypress Trees*
- *Half-Tone*
- *Sunlight and Shadow*
- *The Monterey Coast*
- *Mariposa Big Trees*
- *Yosemite Valley*
- *An Impression*

1905 NEW YORK, NEW YORK
Second American Salon at New York, December, under the auspices of the Metropolitan Camera Club of New York and the Salon Club of America. Catalogue.
- *Sunset on Pacific*
- *Cypress Tree*

SAN FRANCISCO, CALIFORNIA
Third Annual Exhibition of the Guild of Arts and Crafts, Red Room, Hotel St. Francis, December.

WASHINGTON, DC
Washington Salon of Photography.

1907 SAN FRANCISCO, CALIFORNIA
California Camera Club, September 20–?. According to *Camera Craft* magazine, October 1907, p. 462, these pictures had been "exhibited in the East, including New York and other points."

1908 SAN FRANCISCO, CALIFORNIA
Galleries of Vickery, Atkins & Torrey, Exhibition of Photographs by W. E. Dassonville, Photographs of California, October 15–22. One-man exhibition.

WORCESTER, MASSACHUSETTS
Fourth Annual Exhibition of Photographs, Worcester Art Museum, November 1–30. Three photographs by Dassonville.

1909 SAN FRANCISCO, CALIFORNIA
San Francisco Architectural Club, Fifth Exhibition, under the direction of the Architectural League of the Pacific Coast, Monadnock Building, October 18–31. Catalogue. Twenty-six photographs by Dassonville:
- *Mission San Gabriel* (illustrated)

1910 PORTLAND, OREGON
Portland Architectural Club, *Year Book 1910*, published in connection with the Second Annual Exhibition in Portland of the Architectural League of the Pacific Coast held in the Galleries of the Museum of Fine Arts, June 3–19. Catalogue. More than one photograph by Dassonville:
- *Old Mission at Santa Barbara, California* (illustrated)

1915 SAN FRANCISCO, CALIFORNIA
Pictorial Photography Exhibit, Liberal Arts Building, Panama-Pacific International Exhibition. Twelve photographs by Dassonville. Awarded Honorable Mention for his photograph, *Bell, Mission San Juan Capistrano*.

1916 SAN FRANCISCO, CALIFORNIA
Fifth International Photographic Salon, Palace Hotel, under the auspices of the California Camera Club, November 25–December 2. Catalogue.
Three photographs by Dassonville, all portraits. Dassonville was the only photographer on the Jury of Selection; the other jurors were Xavier Martinez, Sadakichi Hartman and Bernard R. Maybeck.

1922 LONDON, ENGLAND
International Exhibition of Professional Photography, Professional Photography Association of Great Britain and Ireland. Probably the same photographs that were shown in the San Francisco exhibit the same year.

SAN FRANCISCO, CALIFORNIA
First Annual International Exhibition of Pictorial Photography under direction of the Pictorial Photographic Society of San Francisco, May 19–June 18. Catalogue.
Portrait of Col. C. E. S. Wood
Portrait
Landscape
Mission San Juan Bautista

1923 SAN FRANCISCO AND OAKLAND, CALIFORNIA
Second San Francisco-Oakland Salon of Photography, August 31–October 7. More than one photograph by Dassonville.
Portrait of William Keith

LOS ANGELES, CALIFORNIA
Seventh International Salon of Pictorial Photography, under the auspices of the Camera Pictorialists of Los Angeles, October 15–November 5. More than one photograph by Dassonville.
Portrait of William Keith

1924 PITTSBURGH, PENNSYLVANIA
Eleventh Annual Pittsburgh Salon of Photographic Art, under the Auspices of the Photographic Section, Academy of Science and Art of Pittsburgh, March 2–31. Catalogue.
Portrait of William Keith
Study in Black and White
Portrait of a Young Lady

TORONTO, CANADA
The Toronto Camera Club, 33rd Annual Salon of Pictorial Photography, Canadian National Exhibition, August 23–September 6. More than one photograph by Dassonville.
Study in Black and White, No. II

SAN FRANCISCO, CALIFORNIA
Third San Francisco International Salon of Photography, October 17–November 23.
Four photographs by Dassonville.

PORTLAND, OREGON
Photographers' Association of the Pacific Northwest, in conjunction with the Photographers' Association of California, November 25–?. Three or more photographs by Dassonville. Awarded silver cup for the best print in all classes, first place for Women's Portraits, and third place for Men's Portraits.

1925 BIRMINGHAM, ENGLAND
Second Midland Salon of Photography, August 29–September 5. Four photographs by Dassonville.

BRIDGE OF ALLAN, SCOTLAND
Second Annual Exhibition, Bridge of Allan and District Photographic Society, Scottish Photographic Federation, April 13–25. More than one photograph by Dassonville.

DALLAS, TEXAS
One-man exhibition, July. The same exhibit was later shown in Newark, New Jersey.

NEWARK, NEW JERSEY
One-man exhibition. Camera Craft, Vol. 32, No. 4, April, p. 208, refers to an exhibition of "over thirty of his pictures on the walls of this club."

1925 SAN FRANCISCO, CALIFORNIA
San Francisco Pictorialist Exhibition, Schwabacher-Frey Company Mezzanine, October 12–24.

1926 LIVERPOOL, ENGLAND
International Circle of Pictorial Photographers' Second Annual Exhibition, April (?).
Portrait of John Muir
Portrait in Black and White

HONOLULU, HAWAII
Hawaii Territorial Fair, September 25–October 2.

SAN FRANCISCO, CALIFORNIA
Pictorial Photographers of San Francisco Fourth International Salon, October 17–31.
Two portraits and an unknown number of landscapes

1927 LOS ANGELES, CALIFORNIA
All American Photographic Salon – Sixth Annual Exhibition, under the direction of the Los Angeles Camera club, October 31–November 20.

1928 SAN FRANCISCO, CALIFORNIA
Paul Elder Gallery, April 2–14.
"Pictorial Photographs of San Francisco."
One-man exhibition.

SAN FRANCISCO, CALIFORNIA
Fifth International Exhibition of Pictorial Photography, held by the Pictorial Photographic Society of San Francisco, Galleries of the California Palace of the Legion of Honor, September 16–October 7. Catalogue.
Ferry Boats
San Francisco Hill Tops
Smoky Morning

1933 WASHINGTON, DC
United States National Museum, Smithsonian Institution, December 1–31. One-man exhibition.

1934 NEW YORK, NEW YORK
Camera Club of New York, February.

NEW ORLEANS, LOUISIANA
First Public Exhibition of the Miniature Camera Club of Louisiana, June.

1935 SAN FRANCISCO, CALIFORNIA
Trainer-Parsons Optical Company, "Dassonville's Sierra Photographs," October 10–25. Listed in The Art World: Art Calendar, *Argonaut*, Vol. 114, No. 3024, October 18, 1935, p. 14. One-man exhibition.

1938 BAKERSFIELD, CALIFORNIA
Bakersfield Camera Club. Exact date unknown.

SAN JOSE, CALIFORNIA
San Jose Camera Club. Exact date unknown.

1939 SAN FRANCISCO, CALIFORNIA
San Francisco International Salon of Pictorial Photography, sponsored by the California Camera Club, M. H. de Young Museum, Golden Gate Park, April 2–30. Catalogue.
Untitled

1940 SAN FRANCISCO, CALIFORNIA
A Pageant of Photography, Palace of Fine Arts, Treasure Island, part of the World's Fair Art Exhibits. Catalogue.
Portrait of John Muir

SAN FRANCISCO, CALIFORNIA
M. H. de Young Museum, April 14–?.
Three-person exhibition with John Paul Edwards and P. Douglas Anderson.

1948 SAN FRANCISCO, CALIFORNIA
Eighth Annual Exhibition of Photography, Bohemian Club, May.

EXHIBITION HISTORY

1977 SAN FRANCISCO, CALIFORNIA
California Pictorialism. San Francisco Museum of Modern Art and traveling, January 7–February 27. Catalogue.
 Study in Black and White, No. II
 Landscape with House
 Portrait of Alvin Langdon Coburn
 Miss W.
 Portrait of William Keith
 Sand Dunes
 Woman in Oxford Cap
 California Landscape
 Trees
 (Grasses) (illustrated)
 Woman in Trees
 Portrait
 Seated Woman
 Winter Landscape
 Rocks and Water
 Wild Flowers
 Landscape
 San Francisco From Telegraph Hill

1989 OAKLAND, CALIFORNIA
Picturing California: A Century of Photographic Genius. The Oakland Museum, August 26–November 5. Catalogue.
 Untitled (illustrated)

1992 SANTA BARBARA, CALIFORNIA
Watkins to Weston: 101 Years of California Photography, 1849–1950. Santa Barbara Museum of Art, February 29–May 31 and traveling. Catalogue.
 Richmond Refinery (illustrated)

1994 SAN MARINO, CALIFORNIA
Pictorialism in California – Photographs 1900–1940. Malibu and San Marino: The J. Paul Getty Museum and The Henry E. Huntington Library and Art Gallery and traveling. September 13–November 27. Catalogue.
 California Landscape (illustrated)
 Grasses (illustrated)
 San Francisco Super-Structure (illustrated)

1997 MINNEAPOLIS, MINNESOTA
After the Photo-Secession. The Minneapolis Institute of Arts, February 8–May 4 and traveling. Catalogue.
 Grasses (illustrated)

Dassonville: Published Photographs

Note: Descriptive titles not written by Dassonville are in parentheses.

1900 *Camera Craft*, Vol. 1, No. 1, May 1900.
   In the Land Fog, p. 28
   Calves, p. 29

1901 *Camera Craft*, Vol. 2, No. 4, February 1901.
   Morning Lights, p. 318

   First San Francisco Photographic Salon, under the auspices of the California Camera Club, January 1901.
   Morning Lights

1902 *Overland Monthly*, Vol. 60, No. 4, October 1902.
   (*Sand Dunes, Carmel*), p. 339
   A Portrait Study, p. 340
   Landscape, p. 341
   A Study in Lighting, p. 342
   In a Dutch Village, p. 343
   Portrait, p. 344
   Portrait of Mr. O. V. Lange, p. 345

   Camera Craft, Vol. 4, No. 3, January 1902.
   A Dutch Fishing Boat, p. 124

   Camera Craft, Vol. 5, No. 6, October 1902.
   O. V. Lange
   Portrait of L. Maynard Dixon

   Second San Francisco Photographic Salon, under the auspices of the California Camera Club and the San Francisco Art Association, Mark Hopkins Institute, January 1902.
   Study of a Nude, p. 18

1904 *Camera Craft*, Vol. 9, No. 5, October 1904.
   (*Portrait Study on Platinum*), p. 189

   Photograms of the Year 1904, London: Dawbarn & Ward.
   Mystery, p. 169
   The Yosemite Falls, p. 173

   Camera Craft, Vol. 9, No. 3, August 1904.
   Miss E., p. 119
   Twilight, p. 124

   Camera Craft, Vol. 9, No. 4, September 1904.
   One illustration, a major portrait; only known copy at International Museum of Photography, George Eastman House.
   Portrait of Alvin Langdon Coburn, frontispiece

   Catalogue of the Guild of Arts and Crafts, San Francisco, December 1904.
   "*Dome*" *Yosemite*

1905 *Sunset (The Pacific Monthly)*, Vol. 14, No. 4, February 1905.
   (*On the Seventeen-Mile Drive, Near Monterey*), frontispiece, p. 392
   (*On the Pacific Grove Peninsula, Overlooking Carmel Bay*), p. 399

   Camera Craft, Vol. 11, No. 2, August 1905.
   Canal Scene – Rotterdam, p. 54
   Sand Dunes – Pacific Grove, p. 75

   Camera Craft, Vol. 10, No. 4, April 1905.
   (*At Carmel-by-the-Sea*), p. 219

   Camera Craft, Vol. 10, No. 5, May 1905.
   (*Carmel-by-the-Sea*), p. 262

1906 *Photograms of the Year 1906*, London: Dawbarn & Ward.
   A Child Reading, p. 153

   Camera Craft, Vol. 12, No. 1, January 1906.
   A Dutch Fishing Boat, p. 3

   Sunset (The Pacific Monthly), Vol. 18, No. 1, November 1906.
   (*A Chimney Corner in Frank Power's House at Carmel-by-the-Sea*), p. 56

1907 *Photograms of the Year 1907*, London: Dawbarn & Ward.
    Point Carmel, p. 98

1908 *Photograms of the Year 1907*, London: Dawbarn & Ward.
    Californian Palms, p. 84

American Annual of Photography 1908,
New York: Tennant and Ward, 1907.
    A California Mission (Pinhole), p. 77

1909 *Year Book – San Francisco Architectural Club, Fifth Exhibition*
(the first held under the auspices of the SFAC).
Annual Exhibition of the Coast League, San Francisco: n.p.
    Mission San Gabriel, p. 20

American Annual of Photography 1909,
New York: Tennant and Ward, 1908.
    The Monterey Coast (California), p. 270
    (Portrait of a Child), p. 287

Camera Craft, Vol. 16, No. 2, February 1909.
    At Mission Santa Barbara, frontispiece

1910 *Portland Architectural Club, Year Book 1910*,
Portland: n.p., 1910.
    (Old Mission at Santa Barbara, California)

1911 Elder, Paul, compiler. *California the Beautiful*,
San Francisco: Paul Elder & Company, 1911.
    (Mount Tamalpais near the Golden Gate), p. 35

1913 Elder, Paul. *The Old Spanish Missions of California*, San Francisco: Paul Elder & Company, 1913.
    Mission San Miguel Arcangel, frontispiece
    Mission San Diego de Alcala, opposite p. 4
    Mission Santa Ines, opposite p. 84

1914 *Sunset (The Pacific Monthly)*, Vol. 33,
No. 2, August 1914.
    Miss Donaldina Cameron, p. 351
    Captioned "Superintendent of the Presbyterian Mission in San Francisco, who during eighteen years of devoted service has rescued hundreds of Chinese slave-girls from their owners."

1915 Sterling, George. *Yosemite – An Ode*,
San Francisco: A. M. Robertson, 1915.
    From Yosemite Falls, frontispiece
    The Yosemite Falls, opposite p. 2
    The Bridal Veil Falls, opposite p. 6
    Twilight, opposite p. 10
    Mornings – The Half-Dome, opposite p. 15

Taylor, Edward Robeson. *In the Keith Room at the Exposition*, San Francisco: Taylor & Taylor, 1915.
    Portrait of William Keith, frontispiece
    (Reproduction of a Painting of a Landscape with Cows by William Keith), p. 2

Murphy, Thomas D. *On Sunset Highways*, Boston:
The Page Company, 1915.
    Entrance to San Luis Rey Cemetery, opposite p. 180
    A Corner of Capistrano, opposite p. 184
    Arches. Capistrano, opposite p. 188
    Arcade. Santa Barbara, opposite p. 200
    Bell Tower. Santa Inez, opposite p. 220
    Interior Church. San Miguel, opposite p. 234
    Arcade. San Miguel, opposite p. 236
    San Carlos Borromeo. Monterey, opposite p. 258
    Carmel Mission, opposite p. 260
    Church and Cemetery. San Juan Bautista, opposite p. 274
    San Antonio de Padua, opposite p. 354
    Ruins of la Purisima, opposite p. 360

Camera Craft, Vol. 22, No. 11,
November 1915.
    Portrait of a Child, frontispiece

Camera Craft, Vol. 22, No. 2,
February 1915.
    The Late John Muir, frontispiece

1916 *Sierra Club Bulletin*, Vol. 10, No. 1, January 1916.
  (*Portrait of John Muir*), frontispiece
  (*Portrait of John Muir*), opposite p. 8
  John Muir, opposite p. 9

San Francisco News Letter and California Advertiser, Christmas Number, December, 1916.
  Portrait of a Young Woman, p. 31

1923 *Photo-Era*, Vol. 51, No. 6, December 1923.
  William Keith, p. 311

Camera Craft, Vol. 30, No. 12, December 1923.
  Portrait of William Keith, frontispiece

1924 *Camera Craft*, Vol. 31, No. 10, October 1924.
  (*The Winning Portrait*) [*Portrait of a Young Girl*], p. 495

1926 *American Photography*, Vol. 20, No. 6, June 1926.
  Study in Black and White, p. 288

1928 *The Russ Building*. San Francisco: The C. A. Horne Co., 1928, Taylor & Taylor, printers. Lavish promotional booklet for the recently completed building.
  (*The Russ Building*), cover

The San Franciscan. Vol. 2, No. 10, October 1928.
  From Portsmouth Square, p. 13
  Captioned "A recent impression of San Francisco's mounting skyline by W. E. Dassonville whose exceptional photographs are recognized as the best pictorial interpretations of the city as she is today."

San Francisco Chronicle, "Photographic Triumphs," Rotogravure Pictorial Section, Sunday, September 30, 1928.
  (*Close to Home*), p. 3
  Captioned "The top deck of a ferry boat affords an interesting composition of lines, shapes and shadows for W. E. Dassonville of San Francisco."

Camera Craft, Vol. 35, No. 12, December 1928.
  Ferry Boats, p. 558

1929 *The San Franciscan*. Vol. 4, No. 6, April 1929.
  San Francisco Silhouettes, p. 19
  Captioned "In which Dassonville's camera has recorded one of the city's Paradoxes."

The San Franciscan. Vol. 4, No. 8, June 1929.
  Proud Elegance Crowns Telegraph Hill, p. 15
  Captioned "The tangle of undergrowth surrounding the old marine look-out has given way to smooth avenues and stately urns where tourists watch the island-strewn bay."

The San Franciscan. Vol. 4, No. 10, August 1929.
  San Francisco. 1929, p. 15
  Captioned "The ever changing skyline of the city at the Portals of the Western Hemisphere as recorded by the photographic artist Dassonville."

1930 *The San Franciscan*. Vol. 5, No. 1, November 1930. One illustration with notation indicating prior publication, June 1929:
  (*Proud Elegance Crowns Telegraph Hill*), p. 8

1931 *San Francisco Chronicle*. Sunday, January 25, 1931 in "Photographic Art Exhibit Continues" under "Notes of Art and Artists."
  (*Labor*), p. D5

1934 *The Camera*. Vol. 68, No. 1, January 1934. Six illustrations from Dassonville's one-man exhibition at the Smithsonian Institution, Washington, DC, 1933:
  The Condensing Tower, p. 23
  Fishing Boats, p. 24
  The Monterey Coast, p. 27
  Thistles, p. 28
  Tide Lands, p. 30
  Sand Dunes, p. 32

1934 *San Francisco Chronicle*, Sunday, April 1, 1934, "Club to See Camera Studies," section CCC.
  (*Silver Birch Trees*), p. 5

1937 *The Argus*. Melbourne, Australia, Saturday, October 9, 1937.
  Untitled (*Gnarled Tree*), cover of art section

1939 *Camera Craft*, Vol. 66, No. 11, November 1939.
  Don Oliver (*Photographing in the Sierra*), frontispiece

1942 Cornelius, Brother, F.S.C., M. A. *Keith – Old Master of California*. New York: G. P. Putnam's Sons, 1942.
  Portrait of William Keith (*facing right*), opposite p. 528
  Self-Portrait, opposite 528
  Portrait of John Muir, opposite p. 545
  Portrait of William Keith, opposite p. 545

1977 *California Pictorialism*. San Francisco: San Francisco Museum of Modern Art, 1977.
  Grasses [*Reeds and Sand*], cover and p. 41

1980 Ferlinghetti, Lawrence, and Nancy J. Peters. *Literary San Francisco*. San Francisco: City Lights and Harper & Row, 1980.
  Portrait of George Sterling, p. 106

1989 *Picturing California: A Century of Photographic Genius* Oakland: The Oakland Museum and Chronicle Books, 1989.
  (*Untitled*) p. 57

1992 *Watkins to Weston: 101 Years of California Photography*. Santa Barbara: Santa Barbara Museum of Art and Robert Rinharts, 1992.
  (*Untitled*) [*Richmond Refinery*], p. 95

1994 Wilson, Michael G., and Dennis Reed. *Pictorialism In California: Photographs 1900–1940*. Malibu and San Marino: The J. Paul Getty Museum and The Henry E. Huntington Library and Art Gallery, 1994.
  California Landscape, p. 30
  Beach Grasses, p. 41
  San Francisco Ferry Super-structure, p. 58

1997 Peterson, Christian. *After the Photo-Secession – American Pictorial Photography, 1910–1955*. Minneapolis and New York: The Minneapolis Institute of Arts and W. W. Norton & Company, 1997.
  Beach Grass, p. 85

"Platinotype Printing"
Camera Craft, Vol. 1, No. 1, May 1900, p. 29

The manipulation of platinotype paper, though very simple, is regarded by many amateurs as an extremely difficult process. The hesitancy and unwillingness to experiment is responsible, more than anything else, for this idea. Platinotype paper is almost as easy to work as the common blue print and as far as simplicity of manipulation is concerned, ranks next in order. It is a paper that possesses unlimited scope for the amateur, and by experiment an individuality in printing may be secured so that in time a print made in a certain tone would always be recognized as your own. In the shadows full detail can be secured, while the shading from the darker to the lighter part of tile print is exquisite. The paper is packed in tin tubes to exclude moisture and is of three grades: A.A., thin and smooth; B.B., heavy, smooth, and C.C., heavy, rough. For general purposes C.C. is to be preferred, as it has a surface somewhat between smooth and rough. There is also a sepia paper, but as its value is limited and its keeping qualities poor, it will not come into general use.

The printing can be done in strong sunlight for strong negatives, or in the shadow for weak ones. Print until the shadows are well out, then immerse in the developing solution. It will take two or three trials to obtain the proper exposure. Development will be complete in about thirty seconds. The print is then transferred, without washing, to a bath composed of muriatic acid, 1 ounce; water, 60 ounces. Two other trays, containing similar baths, should be provided and the prints shifted from one to the other at intervals of five minutes, making three washings in all. After the final clearing bath, wash for thirty minutes and dry.

No developing formula is furnished with the paper, but it can be obtained in packages sufficient to mix fifty ounces of developer. Should the printing be carried too far, the image will, of course, appear too dark; however, prints may often be saved by removing from the solution as soon as the evidence of over-exposure appears. If the print is under-exposed the action of the developer ceases after a certain stage has been reached; therefore it is better to err on the side of over-exposure.

The temperature of the developer is of great importance and has much to do with the tone of the print. By using a cold solution a cold tone is secured, while at a temperature of 200° Fahr., the print has that rich brown tone so very suitable for certain subjects. The normal temperature should be about 80° Fahr.

Under-exposed prints may be intensified after washing in a bath made by adding 10 grains of silver nitrate to a solution composed of hydroquinon, 2 grains; citric acid, 20 grains; water, 1 ounce. The print should be rocked continually, in the tray, until the required density is reached; then fix in a 10% hypo solution.

"Individuality in Photography"
Overland Monthly, Vol. 40, No. 4, October 1902, pp. 339-45

Whether photography is or is not an art is no longer a question. It is. That there are photographers who are not artists is as true as the statement that all painters are not artists. A man or woman who purchases a camera is immediately termed a photographer. This is perfectly correct even as a person who purchases paints, brushes and canvas, and who has a small knowledge of drawing and color is termed a painter.

But neither of them are to be called artists. There are, however, painters who are artists, and in this same sense there are also photographers who are artists.

The work of the greatest photographers such as Demachy, Steichen, Stirling, Kasebier, White and others, has been acknowledged by painters who are artists to be works of art. The jury of the Champs de Mars in Paris for the present year, accepted ten photographs by Mr. Steichen. Does not this individual exhibit of talent brand photography as an art? Yet when these photographs had been accepted, jealousies and political intrigues within the Salon itself proved powerful enough to prevent their being hung, simply because they were photographs. And this shows clearly the attitude of many people towards photographic work.

The rejection of this work after it had been accepted was simply a light by which we could see the prejudices of an old world. It is to be hoped that these prejudices will wear away, and the work of such men as Mr. Steichen and others will be given the attention it merits.

How high photography may go in the field of art still remains to be seen. Art is an expression, and the highest form of this expression must emanate solely from the individual. To glance back at the great number of canvases which have been painted, we find comparatively few of them which stand out from the ordinary, and those few were done by people who individualized themselves.

These few have created the standards of their art by their work, and so have given the art that is to the public, for the public does not give art, but receives it. And this form of art must then necessarily be a creative art the artist must be the re-creator of that which is created.

One who wishes to interpret nature must first go to nature and learn her forms and moods; then, when he has learned this, he re-creates her until she reaches his ideal of an harmonious whole.

This, then, is the highest plane of art, that plane which so few reach. As for photography, it would be ridiculous for it to ever attempt to reach this plane except on a very small scale. A photographer may, however, select those aspects of nature which form a harmony, and having made this selection and photographed it he may so modify his print that the resulting piece of work may be placed at a very high standard.

Whistler, in his "Gentle Art of Making Enemies," remarks: "The painter has the same pencil the sculptor the same chisel of centuries." And in this same sense, the photographers have had but the same cameras and the same plates that they have had for years. Whence, then, comes this improvement? From those few altogether too few who have individualized themselves and made photography an art.

Of course, mechanical or scientific photography is entirely eliminated from this article. It has its value, but this value is entirely foreign to the present subject.

Art is not personal. Whatever we have trained our eyes or ears to receive as beautiful constitutes our form of harmony, and those who have trained themselves, or have been trained (the idea is the same) to the highest forms of harmony are necessarily the greatest critics. Even with the judgment of such critics many would not agree; so judgment on art matters must be largely personal, even as it is on all other matters.

The same sun shines upon the same earth, yet each one of us casts a different shadow.

Thus, in art matters, our opinions are largely personal, yet art proper is neither personal nor individual. That which is true to a single person may not be the truth. It may be true only to that individual. That which is true to all is generally the truth. That we have existed, shall exist and do exist, is the truth; and art in its greatest sense is part of this truth, for it is but the product of the refining of our existence. By this sign do we see that art is not personal.

To individualize oneself is to develop one's individuality. Why cannot this be done in photography as well as in painting? Within the last four years photographers the world over have made vast progress, although the real results of their labor are just becoming evident. When they first began to appear with their landscape work, artists paid them scant courtesy – as they deserved. The work was filled with detail: every branch, twig or leaf was minutely photographed as though its presence was highly essential. Painfully and slowly they had to learn the uselessness of all this. They had to learn that when a certain point in nature was looked at that this detail was not seen. So, gradually, this detail was merged into masses, and those masses made to have their harmonious value. It was at this stage that photographs began to have any art value whatever.

The work at that time was of the "extreme type," as it has been called. But gradually it is settling down to a solid foundation. While photographic art was progressing in the hands of the few, the many – as might be expected – remained antagonistic, even as many are to-day. They complained, largely, that the work was not photographic, but they could better have said that the work was not according to their old ideas of photography. Possibly the new prints were not photographs in the accepted meaning of the word. Still those who were working out their ideas did not care very much whether their work was called photographic or not. They had emotions and ideas to express, so they went ahead steadily regardless of the old school. Their works are not photographs – let us say, for the benefit of those who still hold to the old ideas. Well, does it make any difference? Beauty speaks for itself even without a name.

Those few who worked photography up to its present level have at last revolutionized it.

All that has been said of landscape work is applicable also to portrait work. In portrait photography there are two individualities to be considered – the photographer's and that of the person being photographed. Both should be considered, but this is too seldom the case with some workers who have individualized themselves, and whose work is so strongly stamped with their own individuality as to entirely obliterate that of the person being photographed.

Another great error is to attempt to photograph any two persons in exactly the same manner, for no two persons are alike in either face or general character.

In portrait work above all things to be desired is a likeness of the subject. The composition – in its general sense – is secondary. However, a portrait, if only a portrait, is not a picture in the accepted sense of the word "picture." Those few who have combined with that likeness of the subject an arrangement or composition which has an harmonious relation to the whole have brought photography up to its present standing.

A great question is: "What constitutes a good likeness?" Is it simply an image of the physical form of the face when the face wears a certain expression, or is it something else? Certainly something more, and that indescribable something should be the personality of the subject as it appeals to the photographer. Few have the faculty of grasping this personality, for their senses are too dulled to receive such impressions; oftentimes dulled through the desire to make their business a financial success rather than to have the work proper a success. Both Whistler and Sargent have made their work a success by holding it aloof from a financial basis. The first obstacle which commercial photographers or those who earn a livelihood with photography, had to overcome, was this very one.

The public did not take kindly to their work, for it was so new and so entirely Different from anything which had been produced before that it required some while for many persons to learn to like it. At the present time there are so many who sympathize with the "new school," as it might be termed, that the work is bound to be a success. At a recent photographic exhibit in New York in English art dealer offered three hundred dollars for a single photographic print and the offer was refused – an incident which strongly illustrates the value of good prints.

Amateur photographers who desire to take up photography seriously, with the desire to rise above the ordinary mechanical photographer, would do well to work entirely by themselves until they have mastered the mechanical side, and then go to painters for their criticisms; to go to a photographer for information is to become more deeply tangled in the web of error. This might seem ridiculous, and yet it is true. Mechanical photography is extremely easy, provided one applies oneself to it. Herewith it might well be said in regard to mechanical photography that any one developer is good, any two developers are bad. An over-exposed plate is of as great a value as a normal exposure or an under-exposure, provided you deliberately over-exposed, normally exposed, or under exposed in order to obtain the desired effect. An instrument should always be the Servant of the man, not the master of him. The idea from the standpoint of art should be to give an outward form to an inward emotion.

No matter whether the result be photographic or not, provided you have expressed the emotion you wished to convey, you have accomplished what you wished to do, and the balance of the art training will come of its own accord when you have reached this point. And a beginner would do well not to be bound by inherited ideas, but to think and to work things out for himself, for herein rests his individuality.

"The Manipulation of Platinum Paper"
Camera Craft, Vol. 9, No. 5,
October 1904, pp. 187–190

In an article which appeared in these pages recently, the successful treatment and working of old platinum paper and the saving of over and under-exposed platinum prints was so thoroughly treated that nothing further in that direction seems requisite. It is my purpose in the present paper to set forth the possibilities of the platinum process, treating the subject from a different standpoint upon the regular or "black" papers, colors may be obtained ranging from a very cold to a very warm black. A most beautiful red or green may be secured by simply toning the print; a sepia color can be obtained by the introduction of bichloride of mercury into the developer. Moreover, prints of a greater or less contrast may be made from the same negative by altering the developer, by manipulation in printing and by other means. It is to this side of platinum printing that I shall give my attention.

When it is desired to give to the print that sense of warmth felt in late afternoon and twilight landscapes the sepia color obtained by the hot developer or the use of mercury is best suited. These varying shades of sepia will also be found pleasing for many portraits. The red color is particularly adapted to sketchy effects both in portraiture and in landscapes, suggesting as it does red crayon. The green is not so suitable for landscapes as might be supposed but for marines it probably answers better than any other color.

These formulae have stood the test of my every-day practice for several years. They have in my hands been found the simplest and most suitable of a great number of published formulae which I have given careful trial. Since it is impossible without illustrations to show the exact colors and gradations obtained it would be advisable for the worker wishing to fully avail himself of the processes outlined, to make up a set of prints, showing the different results obtainable from the same negative. Such a set of prints will permit him to make an intelligent selection of the process most desirable in any given case.

Red or Green Prints

To make a red platinotype, proceed as follows, making up three solutions:

No. 1.	Uranium nitrate	48 grs.
	Glacial acetic acid	48 min.
	Water	1 oz.
No. 2.	Potassium ferricyanide	48 grs.
	Water	1 oz.
No. 3	Ammonium sulphocyanide	1/2 oz.
	Water	1 oz.

When ready to use take one part of each solution and add 100 parts of water. In this final solution place a finished print; one developed, cleared and washed.

It will immediately commence to tone to a color termed Bartollozzi red; the longer the print is immersed the darker the color will become. When the desired depth of color has been obtained remove the print, washing it in several changes of water made slightly acid by acetic acid, and then dry.

These acid baths are important since the slightest trace of alkalinity will entirely remove all of the red color leaving the print as it was before being toned. It may be seen by this that should the print be toned too dark it can be cleared of its color by being rinsed in water to which has been added a small amount of any alkali. After this the print may be well washed and again toned to the color desired. When mounting prints which have been toned with nitrate of uranium it is advisable to add a few drops of acetic acid to the paste used.

To produce a green platinotype, tone the print red as just described; rinse in an acid bath and then immerse for a few minutes in a bath of bichloride of mercury; 18 grains to the ounce of water. From this bath the print is transferred, without washing to a solution of trichloride of iron, 10 grains to the ounce of water. In a few minutes the desired color is obtained. The print is then well washed in several acid baths and dried. It is generally supposed that prints treated in this manner are not permanent, but some prints made about four years ago show no signs of deteriorating.

Intensifying Platinum Prints

It often happens that prints when finished are too weak and ordinarily, are thrown away. Such prints are easily saved by intensification. Make a solution of:

Hydroquinone.	2 grs.
Citric acid	60 grs.
Water	3 ozs.

When the chemicals are entirely dissolved add 10 grains of nitrate of silver. The platinum print is placed in this solution and allowed to remain until sufficiently intensified when it is removed given a slight washing and fixed in a weak solution of hypo after which it is well washed and dried.

Sepia Prints by the Use of Mercury

The introduction of bichloride of mercury into the developer changes the resultant color from a black to a sort of sepia. The amount of mercury required depends upon the effect desired and also upon the paper which is used. As a general rule, with the

American platinum, from one quarter to one tenth of a grain to the ounce of developer will be sufficient. With the Willis & Clements' paper from one to one and a quarter grains to the ounce will usually be found necessary. Using greater quantities than these produces a rather disagreeable color and it will also be found that the greater the amount of mercury used the less the half-tones are preserved. Prints treated in this manner have one great drawback: they are permanent only when the iron contained in the paper is entirely removed by the acid baths, but washing the prints in these baths has a very wrong tendency to remove all traces of the sepia color owing to the action of the hydrochloric acid upon the mercury. A print developed in a mercury developer will have lost all its color by the time the iron is entirely removed, if an average strength of acid clearing bath be used.

The only way which I have found to overcome this difficulty is to leave the prints in the developer for at least four minutes, thus giving the mercury plenty of time in which to act, and then clear the prints in three weak acid baths of: muriatic acid, 1 ounce; water, 200 ounces. By following this course the loss of color will be very slight and the iron will be entirely eliminated.

EXTREME CONTRASTS, COLD AND WARM BLACKS

It often happens that for some reason a print very strong in contrast and cold in color is desired. To secure this, the following developer answers admirably:

Neutral oxalate of potash	16 ozs.
Phosphate of potash	4 ozs.
Sulphate of potash	1/2 oz.
Water	100 ozs.

The solution should be used cold and the print immersed as usual. The length of time required to develop is at least five minutes, the image appearing and developing very slowly. After development the prints should be rinsed in the three customary acid baths of: muriatic acid, 1 ounce; water, 50 ounces. In mixing up formulae containing neutral oxalate of potash the oxalate should be first entirely dissolved and the solution then tested with litmus paper. Should it prove acid, neutralize with carbonate of potash; if alkaline, slowly add oxalic acid until neutral.

Another method of securing greater contrast without at the same time producing cold blacks is to place a piece of blue glass over the negative while printing. As it is difficult to procure such glass entirely free from spear points and bubbles it is advisable to paste over one side of the glass a piece of French tissue-paper. With the papered side toward the negative place the glass over the printing-frame, never in contact with the negative. By this means the shadows from the bubbles are prevented and the print will show no mark from them. Using the developers which are supplied by the various manufacturers of platinum paper one generally obtains a medium gray print when they are used at a normal temperature, say 70 degrees Fahrenheit. By heating the developer, even to the boiling point, the color becomes warmer, varying according to the temperature of the solution. The increased temperature of the developer plays another important part by materially reducing the contrast of the print. By holding the print over the steaming solution before developing and until the surface has had an opportunity of becoming slightly moist, a still further decrease in contrast will result. Another method of producing a print with lessened contrast is to remove the paper from the tin the evening before printing and allow it to remain over night without the package of preservative, in a closed drawer. The paper will become slightly dampened and give, when used judiciously, beautiful soft effects without the warm black color produced by the use of a hot developer.

"Recent Development of Photography"
San Francisco News Letter and California Advertiser
Christmas Number 1916, pp. 30–031

It is one of the laws of life that everything either advances or declines. The history of nations no less than individuals has proven this conclusively. To permit of stagnation is to encourage death. This age is still one of advancement, photography amongst the other pursuits. Compare the photographs of Daguerre and his disciples with one of the modern photographs, and the marked progress is marvelous. In what distinction does the difference lie? The trained eye can see at a glance the difference between the two, and it recognizes that in one of the modern prints values of tone and color have been rendered with a precision far nearer to the truth of values than Daguerre ever attained.

The reason for this is not far to seek. The original discovery passed through the stages of wet plate, the dry plate and the rendering of the dry plate sensitive to colors by means of which the Lumiere and other color processes have sprung into existence. The serious investigation into the subject of glass making and the perfection of the Jena glass through which the high power lens came into existence has subscribed its part to the grand total. Yet there has been little done for photography, as such, in all these late years of scientific investigation. Vast sums of money have been spent in the understanding of every industry, but the work of real worth either scientific or commercial along the lines of photography has been unappreciable.

Whence, then, comes our modern photography? Whence comes art? From the hand of those who are capable of executing it, and in these the advancement lies.

Within the last fifteen years there has arisen a series of both men and women, formed in some cases into schools, such as Clarence H. White has inaugurated in the East, who have endeavored to break away from tradition and offer in place of the typical harsh, hard photograph some expression containing imagination, beauty of form and rendering of values. These few real students have each in their way succeeded. The road has been rough, as all new roads unbeaten and untrod are bound to be. Yet for all the difficulties, much has been accomplished in making photography one of the arts, and gradually it is becoming recognized as such.

However, in all matters pertaining to Art the difficulty in securing recognition lies fundamentally in the public's opinion of the process used. Those arts which have their base in a mechanical medium are classified as graphic arts, and their entrance into the fine arts is forbidden. The Panama-Pacific Exposition took this stand, and so photography, absolutely regardless of *its* results was barred from the Fine Arts Building, while paintings (one might say regardless of *their* results), were admitted. The resuit in many cases was a compliment to photography.

In its final analysis the camera registers the result which a trained individual arranges before it, becoming, as it were, the mechanical draftsman. It has no creative power of its own as the brush of the artists may be said to have, and the plate is beyond argument a mechanical result. But the alterations which can and are made in the plate, and the latitude and alterations possible by printing the plate in such mediums as bichromated gum and pigment colors, surely raises it as an art far above the designation of graphic arts. And it was the result of all the foremost workers in the medium of photography feeling this way that precluded their sending examples of their prints to our recent exposition, a matter greatly to be regretted, since it kept the public from seeing exceptionally beautiful work which has been welcomed at all the great European Expositions.

It is to be expected that with nature about us always in colors, that every individual, both the general public as well as artists, should keenly feel the absence of actual color in the photographic prints. The basis of color according to a certain theory lies in the three primary colors, and it is through this means that many ingenious endeavors have been made to produce photographs in their actual colors.

Their success has been only relative. The Lumiere process, which consists in coating starch grains with each of the primary colors in separate lots, mixing the dried grains and coating on glass, and again coating this prepared surface with the sensitive emulsion so that by exposing through the back of the plate a color separation is produced, is perhaps the best one on the market to-day. In any event, it has the advantage that the colors possess substance and feeling after the manner of oil paintings, while the other processes are weak with the distinct feeling of the aniline dyes.

The fact that the prints are on glass is a great hindrance – and so far it has been impossible to transfer them to paper. It might be said, speaking in a broad manner, that nothing has been done in color photography in the true sense of the word.

An interesting development of the Art of Photography is shown in the few guilds or clubs formed for the purpose of mutual exhibitions of the highest class of work. New York possesses such a center. Mr. Alfred Stieglitz has established it in the heart of the city, where in "The Little Galleries," as he calls the rooms, periodical exhibitions are given by the members of this "Photo Secession" club, and occasionally paintings are also included. Individually, Mr. Stieglitz has probably worked harder and more sincerely for the general advancement of the work than any other American.

Europe has not kept pace with us in progress. I believe it safe to make the statement that the whole modern movement is distinctly American and had its origin here. There are, however, among the European amateurs some of the most proficient workers in the art of photography that are known. Their prints are truly marvelous, but the professional photographer in Europe has not kept pace with these men. Possibly this is due to the fear of commercial disaster, or it may be the result of years of training along the lines of old traditions.

"Projection vs. Contact Printing"
Camera Craft, Vol. 30, No. 11,
November 1923, pp. 542–543

I am not going to hold a brief for projection nor for contact printing. In the final analysis, as I see the matter, you have a series of gradation represented in the negative, that is the plate with which you are going to get the gradation in your print. By gradation I do not mean the number of gradations as shown by a gradation meter, but from the standpoint of tone value. If you have a value in the negative, it will print out where the whites are not blocked out, and you will get a very charming print by contact. Furthermore, if you stand entirely for projection, you have eliminated platinum entirely, you have eliminated carbon, and you have eliminated gum printing, some of the most interesting photographic items in the art. Now, if you go into projection, so far as material to use is concerned, you have come into a very narrow field. There are very few papers to select from, and these few are, broadly speaking, alike. You are limited in the material you have to use, but you have gained one point, you have gained the power of producing the exact effect which you may desire, by selection and manipulation, and the luminous quality in your print is gained easily. But that same luminous quality is gained in contact printing. By working with a large plate you may gain the quality in that negative that you wish, and in the final print from that negative by contact you may get the same identical effect which you gain by projection. Let us consider projection as a thing by itself, irrespective of an argument between contact printing and projection. There is no argument as to whether a painter uses a sash tool or some other brush. Now, I think the thing most needed today – and a subject which I have myself worked on very diligently for the last three years is really high grade, fine enlarging papers, sensitive enough to use for enlarging. This is a subject very near to my heart; it has this advantage over the contact printing, that you are not burdened with a heavy kit. If you are working in a studio your average waste is about fourteen plates out of fifteen and if you are using 8x10 plates for contact work or 5x7 for projection, your bills at the end of the month are quite different. I think myself it is a real answer from the standpoint of real economy. I find this great difficulty in papers used for projection; if you take the bromide, the very fast papers, and you use a light powerful enough to see clearly what you are doing, then the papers are so sensitive that you have difficulty in exposing them uniformly, for the moment you stop down you have overcome your diffusion. So that the ideal type of enlarging paper is slow in character rather than fast, and also slow enough to stand from three to five or seven seconds. If you can get uniform results, projection has much value, particularly from the point of view of economy. But, from the standpoint of art in photography, I cannot hold a brief for projection as against contact printing. I, myself, working with an open stop, have secured negatives on paper coated by myself that have all the charm, all the softness, all the quality of diffusion in the positive which may be gained by projection. Projection has real value in that your control and the actual time of printing may have considerable latitude. The big thing is to get the negative so that it will print and give you what you want, and the method of projection or contact printing is merely an instrument for getting what you want.

"The Metric System"
Camera Craft, Vol. 31, no. 2,
February, 1924, pp. 94–96

I know it is customary to begin a talk of this sort with the words, "Ladies and Gentlemen, Fellow Members of the Association" and so on. That expression is not natural with me, so I am going to use exactly the words I would like to use, and I am going to say – Fellow Craftsmen: I feel that an Association, a group of people, are only strong so long as they serve a purpose. When they cease to serve a purpose, they become weak. And, when Miss Dahl spoke to me about the possibility of my giving a series of talks to you, I laid out in my mind various things that, at one time or another, I have wanted to know, things that I have found most valuable in my work, and I decided that I would arrange those things in order that there might be some purpose in my talk.

The first thing that we are going to speak of, tonight, is dry, unutterably dry; it is going to be difficult to present to you. But I can assure you that, if you can get into your minds the idea that I wish to convey to you, you will have a bigger, broader understanding of photography; you will be able to diminish your cost of doing business, you will be able to work more rapidly and more efficiently; and your results will be definite, and you will surely be able to find your way out of many troubles because, if there is any field in which it can truthfully be said that knowledge is power, it is in the field of photography.

In my own endeavors to understand the nature of photographic chemistry, I found very little in the printed literature; and when I tried to fathom some parts of photography, I found that, wherever I turned, I had to have a certain knowledge, a certain foundation, before I could get anywhere. Photographic books were lacking in that particular knowledge. It is that foundation which we will deal with, in particular tonight. I have found that, in many cases, photographers do not understand what is meant by "per cent," so I am going to tell you something about what a per cent solution means.

We have three distinct weights and measure tables: We have the Troy system, the Apothecary and the Avoirdupois. Photographic formulae are in Avoirdupois, which gives 437.5 grains to an ounce.

Now, for the purpose of understanding the per cent system, we first take a graduate or other vessel for containing a liquid, one which will hold 100 ounces. Then we take, according to the Avoirdupois system, 437.5 grains, say of bromide of potash, and put that ounce in the vessel and dissolve it, and then fill it right up to the 100 ounce point. We then have put one ounce into a hundred ounces of water; and that is a one per cent solution. Or, if we had just put in ten ounces with the same amount of water, we would have a ten per cent solution. That, in other words, means that one-tenth of that solution contains one-tenth of the amount of that substance that is in solution. So, if we wish to take out half an ounce of the substance in the case of the one per cent solution, we take half of it, or fifty ounces of our liquid, and know positively that we have the correct amount. So if we want a quarter of an ounce of the substance, we take twenty-five ounces of the one per cent solution.

It is customary with us to speak in terms of ten per cent, so that by taking ten ounces of a ten per cent solution – remembering that a ten per cent solution is ten ounces of the substance to a hundred ounces of water, we get one ounce of the substance to ten ounces of water, which is also a ten per cent solution, the multiple being the same. So it is customary to make up ten ounces of a solution containing one ounce of the substance and call it a ten per cent solution.

But, if you want to get a definite number of grains, you have a job on your hands. For example, in a solution of that character, 437.5 grains in ten ounces of water, how are you going to get out ten grains. I got brain fag out of it. And that is the real, honest reason why so many of us have not any technical knowledge – because you don't know your weights and measures. It is just a great, big mix up. By proportioning the number of grains to the liquid or vice versa, this can be adjusted, but it is still unwieldy.

Let us forget this system of ours and examine the metric system. It makes no difference what scientific journal you pick up, British, French, Russian, German or American – all that group have taken the metric system for their work; every formula is written in the metric system. How simple it is, how easily operated, and how much it will mean to you when you have it! I do not know whether you are familiar with the character of the system. Broadly speaking, the metric system is identical with the dollar and cent system of our country.

This one hundred cubic centimeter graduate for example, is a multiple of ten or a thousand. This is a Litre. Now, here is my block of weights. They are arranged in sequence so that it makes no difference what per cent you want, it is easily gotten. Now, one gram equals fifteen grains (not accurate). So when I pick up this little fellow I pick up fifteen grains. I will write a formula and show you how the per cent system works out.

Water a hundred cubic centimeters. We are going to take half a per cent of metol, which is .5, that is half a gram. Four times as much hydroquinone, which is 2. or two grams, which as you note is one weight. We want, say two and a half per cent of sulphite, that is 2.5; and we are going to investigate, as a matter of interest, the amount of carbonate, we would like to use. We will add just one gram of carbonate, so carbonate 1. and test it. Add another and test it. Say we carry it to three. So, when we are through, we have written down a definite chemical formula; and if we find then that we want to mix up a larger quantity, all we do for example, is this: multiply by ten each line thus:

Water	100.00
Metol	5.00
Hydroquinone	2.00
Sulphite	2.50
Carbonate	2.00

Multiplied by ten:	
Water	1000.00
Metol	50.00
Hydroquinone	20.00
Sulphite	25.00
Carbonate	20.00

So you see you can easily get somewhere, and know definitely what you are doing. Read in cents and the whole basis will come before you.

The question comes in: How are you going to convert a formula over into the metric system? Take this down on paper. It is frequently, in fact, generally, published erroneously. When you have taken these figures and I have told you how you can convert over to the metric system, you will be surprised how rapidly you will be able to work.

Dry substance: Liquid:
1 oz.=28.35 grams   1 oz.=29.57 c.c.
1 lb.=453.59 grams   16 oz.=473.18 c.c.
1 gm.=15.4324 grains 1 gal.=3785. c.c.

The great difficulty in trying to convey the idea to one's hearers is that one is apt to be rather heedless of telling them exactly what they want to know. Possibly this will help. We will take, for instance, a typical formula:

32 oz. Water
1/2 oz. Metol
2 oz. Hydroquinone
3 1/4 oz. Sulphite
2 oz. Carbonate

Now, say that you want to convert that over into the metric system. We have first the 32 oz., that is a quart. We find that 473 x 2, (16 oz. two times) equals 946 c.c. We have 1/2 oz. of Metol; 1 oz. was 28. Half of that will be 14 grams. Four times that – 56 Hydroquinone. The Sulphite, 8 1/2 oz. We know that each ounce is 28, so 3 1/4 times 28 will make 91 grams; and we have Carbonate 2 oz. which will make 56 grams. So we have converted that formula into the metric system. It is not as readable on that point as I personally would make it. I would put that in proportion so that it would read 1000. Dry substances are grams and liquid cubic centimeters. If you want to make up a smaller quantity, point off one decimal, and the formula is at once just as accurate as in the full amount.

By the use of the metric system, you can cut down your cost of operating and learn to think without confusion, which is a tremendous benefit; and then you can shift your formula back and forth, which may also be a very important help.

As to the temperature for mixing chemicals, it is important when you are making up a definite per cent of solution. Put the dry chemical into the vessel and then add some water, enough to dissolve. After solution, add the required quantity. Remember that water contracts and expands according to whether it is cold or hot. So that, if you wish to make a careful per cent solution, the temperature at the time of pointing off is of the utmost importance. It is better to leave the solution till the following morning before adding the final amount of water; then you can read it off accurately. The temperature for using a developer is about sixty-five degrees (65° Fahrenheit. In use the temperature is far more important than you may think. Take a piece of paper, expose and develop. Then chill the developer down on a block of ice and then try to make another print. You will be astonished. Accurate knowledge is a tremendous short-cut. I use distilled water for my solutions; it is worth while; they last and are effective much longer.

Each chemical in a developer has a definite, fixed result. Metol gives a great deal of gradation. Hydroquinone gives a great deal of density and little gradation. Mix the two and you get both qualities. Sulphite is used to prevent oxidization. Hydroquinone is perfectly useless when the temperature drops down; then the Metol has to do all the work. Metol is not a density giving developer. I am not certain whether we are not using twice as much Hydroquinone as we need. In such thought is where economy lies.

Never get less sulphite then carbonate in your developer. Keep carbonate out of the developer until just before you want to use it, and it will last much longer.

I do not believe, myself, that photographers do not want to know; I honestly believe that they want to know; but there has been that awful haze of weights and measures that has kept them from proper thinking.

Think seriously of the possibilities of the metric system. It will increase, without any effort on your part, the actual amount of work that you can do today, and it will give you accuracy, and you will be reasonably sure of the weight of a thing. Our present system is far more wasteful than you think.

If we could get the rest of the Photographic Associations of America to petition all manufacturers of photographic materials to write their formulae in the metric system, we would have done a great work.

"Photographic Plates and Papers"
Camera Craft, Vol. 31, No. 4,
April 1924, pp. 194–195

The discussions which we have had so far tonight, touching as they did those things so vital to photographers, show to me the rare possibilities of our Photographers' Association of California.

Mr. Webb's splendid demonstration also has a practical value to us which further proves the value of these meetings.

But now I am going to bore you with a lot of things which have no practical use, and yet will, I think, be of interest.

We are going to consider the construction of photographic papers, and certain things about them, with which, possibly, you have not come in contact.

I shall not speak of developing agents – that part of the announcement was a mistake on my part – for the subject will be left for Mr. Van Sicklen to treat with at a later date.

Today, as you know, we are practically all using developing papers. They are emulsion papers; and they are divided into two broad groups – the Chloride papers and the Bromide papers. There is also an intermediary group termed the ChloroBromide papers. The idea exists in the minds of many photographers that the Bromide papers are the very fast papers and the Chloride papers are the very slow ones. That does not follow, as there is a group of Chloride papers that are fast and the Bromide papers which are slow; however, the Chloride papers cannot be made nearly as fast as the Bromide papers when real speed is desired – on the other hand, the Bromide papers were supposed to have a great deal of gradation and lack of contrast. This really was the case for some years after emulsions were used – but today, that is no longer the case, for with our present understanding of emulsions we can shift the gradation of emulsion so that long gradation chloride or short gradation bromide papers can be readily made. From a standpoint of gradation there is no reason why a chloride or bromide paper should reign supreme above the other. When the papers are being made they do not merely take chloride of silver and put it into the emulsion, but the chloride of silver is made right then and there within the emulsion. As an illustration of that, I have brought the chemicals that I used for the purpose. There are three halogens used, chlorine, bromine and iodine. When the emulsion is to be made nitrate of silver is the base for the silver and say sodium chloride for the chlorine. By mixing solutions of these two the chloride of silver will be made. Here we have a solution of sodium chloride. The very moment that silver nitrate is added to the solution, chloride of silver will be formed. The sodium base will attach itself to the nitrate from the silver nitrate and that will remain in solution. We will try the experiment in this tube. You will note the silver chloride formed immediately and how it rapidly falls to the bottom of the tube. This silver chloride is almost insoluble in water, although slightly so. As you know, it is soluble in hypo and the rapidity with which it dissolves is quite surprising. We will dissolve it with hypo by just adding a few crystals. You will notice the rapidity with which it dissolves.

Next we will produce bromide of silver. For this purpose we take potassium bromide solution and drop some nitrate of silver solution into it. You will observe that it is slightly more yellow than our last solution, and again, there is a sinking of the solid mass to the bottom of the glass. This also is soluble in hypo.

These two substances are the bases of practically all of the papers that you use today, and I venture to say that a large part of the papers used today are mixtures of these two.

When we come to examine the iodide we find that it is not fully soluble in hypo. You can note that the idode of silver is distinctly a yellow compound. Its presence in photographic papers can be seen in the daylight. The emulsion is of a distinctly canary color. This I understand is used in the making of dry plates. I do not know that for myself. There is very little literature on the subject of emulsions, and that which is published is likely to be misleading and unreliable.

Now, here in addition to water – for water alone was used in our first three tests – we have some gelurine dissolved in the water. We will add a little of our bromide solution to that jelly solution, shake it and now add some silver nitrate so we have bromide and silver in a gelatine mixture. You note that when the silver is added you don't see those heavy masses. We will have before us just a slightly opalescent photographic emulsion. Of course, it has not been carefully compounded as is a photographic emulsion and as yet it contains very little silver, but we will build it up by adding more. That is the substance you see on your plates and papers when working them. Had I performed this experiment in the dark and then exposed the emulsion to the light and added a photographic developer it would have darkened.

This only touches the very outriders of the photographic processes; but it has this value to you, I think, that it gives you some idea of your materials. So far as the actual physical paper upon which the emulsion is placed, it has these characteristics. It has color, it has weight and it has texture. That is the base upon which the photographic print has to rest. We print on it; and there we are met by these considerations – the gradation that we wish, and also this very important point which is easily overlooked – the depth of the deposit, and, lastly, the speed. The depth of the deposit can easily confuse you. If the depth is not very great, and the paper is of a harsh type possessing very little gradation, the print will show up soft. The reason is that with lack of depth you do not get contrast, and when contrast is lacking flatness comes in. I puzzled over that for many weeks when I first came upon it. I got short scale papers with great softness, but I was not getting density – and that was the answer. The character of the emulsion harsh or soft, the physical type of the paper, whether or not the speed suits our purpose constitutes the problem.

Now concerning the use of developers. The emulsion may be what you want but it does not always follow that you will get the sort of prints you want or expect. You may take a certain developer and get a harsh print, but it does not necessarily follow that it is a harsh paper. It is only relatively so. It depends upon how the developer is made up, whether you produce harsh or soft results. You might have gotten a soft print with exactly the same emulsion. I have known a developer to give great strength when used with a Hammer plate, but be perfectly useless on an Eastman film.

Temperature is also a great factor, and that is where we are likely to find difficulty.

There is a great latitude in the papers and plates which we can all take advantage of if we will study carefully the developer which we are actually using.

In answer to questions, Mr. Dassonville said :

Question – is it advisable to use hot water to dissolve hypo ?

Answer – There is no need to use hot water in dissolving hypo. It will dissolve in a few minutes if contained in a piece of cheese-cloth suspended above and partially immersed in cold water. This plan has the advantage of eliminating all the coarse dirt.

Question – Does warming the developer aid in developing an undertimed plate ?

Answer – Warm developer will help to develop an undertimed plate, but there will be a tendency to fog. Bromide would counteract the tendency to fog which might be brought about by the heat.

Question – Is intensification advisable ?

Answer – When the negative cannot be made over and is so thin that it cannot be printed an excellent intensifier is the bichromate of potash formula.

By varying the strength of the solution more or less intensification can be gotten. The negative is first bleached and then washed and finally developed in daylight. The process can be repeated if the first deposit is not sufficient – "A" gives the least and "B" the greatest amount of deposit.

	A	B	C
Potassium Bichromate	5grs.	10grs.	10grs.
Hydrochloric Acid (Specific gravity 1.1878)	1min.	5min.	20min.
Water	1oz.	1oz.	1oz.

"The Art of Photography"
Camera Craft, Vol. 31, No. 4,
April 1924, pp. 194–195

Fellow Members: It seems my lot when addressing you to try to make a rather intangible thing tangible, and that is again true tonight. We are going to try to speak on "The Art of Photography", – rather complex, because it is a very difficult thing to define. To define Art is difficult; and I rather thought, before the meeting tonight, that if I could settle upon some simple definition of Art, as applied to photography, we might build a conclusion from the definition, and so simplify matters. Therefore, I am going to offer to you tonight, as a definition, this: "An harmonious arrangement of form and mass in correct value." When it comes to sound, our ears will instantly recognize harmony, but our eyes do not recognize harmony of form with the same ease – certain training is necessary.

There are certain fundamental rules of harmony. Particularly is that true in landscape photography, where the lines are very simply marked in their relative position and area. In portraiture, it becomes more complicated, particularly in group arrangement, where you have circles to consider and harmony of form in other relationships. I have brought along a few of my own prints to illustrate some of the points I want to make.

If a tree trunk or larger mass should split the picture quite squarely in the middle – a very common fault in landscape photography – it is almost impossible to produce an harmonious arrangement.

When we get our center object to the side, we get a sense of general proportion, and we can begin to arrange our composition, because the arrangement is flexible. You can then begin to introduce trunks of trees and forms or whatever you want and get a relationship of spaces and a sense of harmony comes in.

The matter of areas is most important. This is a matter which I learned, with a great deal of interest, from a painter friend of mine a great many years ago. He was attempting to explain to me the nature of masses. Getting out three coins of the same area – three dollars – he arranged them as a triangle, then he took away one of the dollars and put a fifty cent piece in its place, then a twenty-five cent piece for the other dollar. By shifting these three pieces into various positions he rapidly illustrated the relationship of areas.

It is an interesting thing as to what constitutes the optical center of a print. It is almost the center of the principal light mass. The optical center of the light is the proper center of the picture. The painters, of course, have the great difficulty that they have added color to their scheme; we have nothing but black and white.

When Mr. De Gaston spoke before the Association I was unable to be present, but in reading his notes I saw something that interested me. It was that photographers today pay too much attention to the paper which they use. This is correct from the point of view from which Mr. De Gaston was speaking but from another point of view it can safely be said that it is impossible to pay too much attention to the paper upon which the print is to be made.

To illustrate what I mean I have here a portrait of John Henry Nash, one of the big American printers. The print is on his own paper which he had made by hand in Holland, it is very rough. You cannot conceive of using it for a woman's or a child's portrait. But there cannot be a lovelier paper for a man's head, big, broad. It is impossible to pay too much attention, actual attention, to the paper which you use, or to say how much the very character of the paper can enter into the making of a portrait and give a broad sketchy feeling to it. You cannot get such a portrait on a smooth paper. It is absolutely impossible for a woman's portrait, which should be on a smoother paper.

"The Business of Photography"
Camera Craft, Vol. 31, No. 5,
May 1924, pp. 242–244

The great evolution that is going on in photography today is one that I think very few photographers are thoroughly conscious of. The day of twelve photographs as an order has gone by, the day of six photographs is here, the day of three photographs to an order is closely advancing, and it follows that a large percentage of orders will presently be for one photograph. Study your costs carefully and prepare yourselves for diminishing orders.

The public are quite aware that the modern portraits are finer today than ever before. They are prepared in many cases to pay as much for six prints as they used to pay for twelve.

The smallest order must show a profit and the photographer should know what the work really costs. This knowledge would give him the courage to charge more.

In my own studio the average person for the last two years has been ordering six. Out of every fifty people I photograph I venture to say that thirty-five order six prints; a few order one print and a very few order one, two, three or four dozen. Reorders are, of course, frequent, but the person who orders just one print from me must show me a profit.

Let each one of you imagine that he or she is to go into partnership with me; that each of us is to put up the sum of $2500.00 so that our capital is $5000.00.

Let us keep down our cost as far as possible in considering how much space we need.

We want an office, nothing very elaborate, so we take a space, say 16x20. We are going to have a dark room in which we shall do our printing and developing, say 12x14. We must have another workroom for storing our stuff, etc., say 12x14. Then we shall require a dressing room, 6x8. For our studio we shall require a larger room, say 15x22. Now we are going to calculate on the square feet, which is 1034 square feet.

The next point – there are two sides to the next point – is how much can we afford to pay for that studio? That is going to be determined by the volume of business we are expecting to do. The neighborhood must be selected accordingly. Let us assume the rental will be 15 cents a square foot. That equals $155.00 a month. In selecting this neighborhood we are not interested in selling prints at $75.00 to $100.00 per dozen; we are going to supply people who spend at the outside from $25.00 to $30.00. In a studio of this sort the average sale is perhaps less than $20.00. Since we could very easily go out and invest at 6 per cent our $5000.00, we ought to get in from our own business at least 10 per cent. Therefore our capital should give us an income of $500 a year.

We select our space, take a five-year lease, run partitions, decorate, put in electric lights and so invest $1000.00 under the head of permanent equipment. This sum must be accounted for at the end of our five-year lease, and so it represents a depreciation expense of $200.00 a year, or $17.00 a month. Therefore our real rent is $155.00 plus $17.00, or $172.00.

Then we have to get our cameras. We will say we spend for lenses and plate holders and general equipment $1000.00. At the end of our five years it is safe to assume that our $1000.00 is not worth over $500.00; divide that by five and by twelve and we bring it down to $8.50 a month on account of depreciation. Also we have insurance and several miscellaneous charges that are going on all the time and making up the sum total of our minimum overhead per month. We have here $172.00 for rent, $8.50 for depreciation, and a general charge for telephone service, towel service, janitor service, and insurance that will undoubtedly run up to $20 per month; and with electric light replacement and other small items we must consider ourselves very lucky if we get off for that. So that we are traveling right along under a fixed overhead of $200.00 a month. If we each draw out $200.00 a month that brings the amount up to $400.00 more. So there are $600.00 outgo to that point. On an average, material charges would be fairly high; but material charges fall down in per cent as the selling price of photographs rises. For example, if we make portraits for $100.00 a dozen our material charge may be 10 per cent; but, if we make them at $20 per dozen, it may rise up to 20 per cent. We have assumed that $20.00 is our average income per person. If we figure on $4.00 of this as material that leaves $16.00. We have to take in $600.00; and we have to take in another $8.50 to take care of our interest charge (we have a $600.00 interest charge, or $8.50 per month), which brings it up to, say, $609.00. Divide that by 16 (price less material) and we find that we have to make thirty-eight engagements a month, each one spending $20.00, in order to meet that overhead-thirty-eight people, $16.00 a month.

Now if we have made this analysis first

FIGURE 22.
Brochure for Dassonville
Charcoal Black papers,
ca. 1945.

and looked into our neighborhood, we might stop to wonder if we could get thirty-eight engagements a month that would average that; because we would realize that a certain percentage of these would not order. To get those thirty-eight orders we might have to handle forty-five people a month, and we would find ourselves up against a pretty substantial business trying to get a 10 per cent guaranteed payment on that $5000.00. If we know all this and find that $20.00 is not enough, we would put it up to $25.00.

Another point of view is: We found that our rental charge was $172.00 a month, and we have here called it an even 1000 feet, or 17 cents a foot. At 17 cents a foot, the two biggest floor spaces are the studio and office. The big cost of a photographic studio lies not in the workroom as such. It lies in the room where you get that business and that room where the first function of the business is fulfilled, a point that very few photographers understand, where very few know how to put a suitable price on their work. At three prints per person you will realize that the cost of the floor space for dressing room and these other items of interest and material – plus some profit – should be covered by a deposit.

We have a fixed rule in my place, and no one ever takes any exception. We mail an engagement card, and we state on the engagement card that a deposit is requested. It is an endeavor to show some profit for my work.

Now, if you are going into a speculative business it is a different matter. But the great business group do not speculate with their businesses. And yet the photographer, if requested, will speculate and may receive no return for his labor.

Does that cover the ground? Can we make a go of it? I was told today – and it amused me very much – by Mr. Magnus: "There is one thing I like about your talk – you know when to quit!" I am through. (Laughter and applause.)

President Morton: Mr. Dassonville has shown very great versatility in the four lectures which he has given to this association, and I thank him very much. Mr. Zinn has asked Mr. Dassonville to attend the convention in Portland and to deliver his talks as part of the convention programme.

[104   WILLIAM E. DASSONVILLE

Selected Bibliography

Adams, Ansel and Mary Austin. *Taos Pueblo.* San Francisco: Ansel Adams, 1930.

Adams, Ansel. *The Making of Forty Photographs.* Boston: Little Brown & Co., 1983.

Adams, Ansel, with Mary Street Alinder. *An Autobiography.* Boston: Little Brown & Co., 1985.

American Photography, Vol. 27, No. 1, 1933, p. 62. Boston: American Photographic Publishing Co.

The Amercan Annual of Photography, 1900–1940. New York: The American Annual of Photography, Inc.

Anderson, Timothy J., Eudorah M. Moore, and Robert W. Winter, editors. *California Design 1910.* Pasadena: California Design Publications, 1974.

Bennett, Jeanne E. "First American Salon." *Camera Craft*, Vol. 10, No. 1, 1905.

Blumann, Sigismund. "Charcoal Black: A New and Different Photographic Paper." *Camera Craft*, Vol. 31, No. 5, 1924.

Brigman, Anne. Letter to Alfred Stieglitz, February 19, 1907. Archives of California Art, Oakland Museum, Oakland, California.

California Art and Architecture, 1911–1935.

The Camera: The Photographic Journal of America, Vol. 4, No. 4, 1931. Philadelphia: Frank V. Chambers.

The Camera, The Photographic Journal of America, Vol. 76, No. 1, 1948, p. 24. Philadelpha: Frank V. Chambers.

Camera Craft, 1900–1941. San Francisco: The Camera Craft Publishing Co.

Clute, Fayette J. "Work in the Western States." *Photograms of the Year*, 1907.

Corn, Wanda. *The Color of Mood: American Tonalism 1880–1910.* San Francisco: M. H. de Young Memorial Museum and the California Palace of the Legion of Honor, 1972.

Cornelius, Brother, F.S.C., *M. A. Keith – Old Master of California.* New York: G. P. Putnam's Sons, 1942.

Cornelius, Brother, F.S.C., *M. A. Keith – Old Master of California*, Vol 2. Moraga, California: St. Mary's College, 1957.

Crocker-Langley San Francisco City Directory, 1890–1941. San Francisco: H. S. Crocker Co.

Danforth, Roy Harrison. "At the Exposition." *The American Annual of Photography*, Vol. 30, 1916.

Dassonville, Donald. "William E. Dassonville: Photographic Artist." May 31, 1985.

Dassonville Papers. Correspondence and ephemera from the estate of William E. Dassonville. Private Collection.

Davie, Helen L. "The Los Angeles Exhibition, Its History and Success and Those Responsible for It." *Camera Craft*, Vol. 4, No. 3, 1902.

Edwards, John Paul. "The San Francisco-Oakland Salon." *Photo Era*, Vol. 41, No. 6, 1923. Boston: Wilfred A. French.

Ennis, Philip. "Photography: San Francisco Firm Makes the Famous Charcoal Black." *San Francisco Chronicle*, November 10, 1940.

Ehrens, Susan. *A Poetic Vision: The Photographs of Anne Brigman.* Santa Barbara: Santa Barbara Museum of Art, 1995.

Elder, Paul, compiler. *California the Beautiful.* San Francisco: Paul Elder & Co., 1911.

Elder, Paul. *The Old Spanish Missions of California.* San Francisco: Paul Elder & Co., 1913.

Ferlinghetti, Lawrence and Nancy J. Peters. *Literary San Francisco: A Pictorial History from its Beginnings to the Present Day.* San Francisco: City Lights Books and Harper & Row, 1980.

Frankenstein, Alfred. "Around the Art Galleries." *San Francisco Chronicle*, April 14, 1940.

Genthe, Arnold "The Third San Francisco Salon." *Camera Craft*, Vol. 7, No. 6, 1903.

Gernsheim, Helmut and Allison. *The History of Photography from the Camera Obscura to the Beginning of the Modern Era*. New York: McGraw-Hill Book Co., 1969.

Herzig, Susan, and Paul M. Hertzmann. Interview with Phiz Mezey, November 1, 1998.

Herzig, Susan, and Paul M. Hertzmann. Notes on William Dassonville from Conversations with Donald Dassonville, October 24–26, 1997; letters from Donald Dassonville, August 31, 1997 and October 27, 1998.

Hussey, Henry A. "The San Francisco-Oakland Salon 1923." *Camera Craft*, Vol. 30, No. 10, 1923.

Innes, Homer William. *Alfred Stieglitz and the Photo-Secession*. Boston: Little Brown & Co., 1983.

Jerome, Lucy. "Artists Flit to Vale and Mountain." *San Francisco Call*, June 6, 1909.

Jerome, Lucy. "In the Art World." *San Francisco Call*, April 4, 1909.

Lokke, Janet. "Dassonville," 1981. Dassonville Papers.

Lokke, Janet. "W. E. Dassonville: The Photographer as Artist," circa 1981. Dassonville Papers.

Mechlin, Leila. "Notes of Arts and Artists." *Sunday Star*, December 17, 1933. Washington, DC.

Murphy, Thomas. D. *On Sunset Highways*. Boston: The Page Co., 1915.

Newhall, Nancy. *Ansel Adams: The Eloquent Light*, Vol. 1. San Francisco: The Sierra Club, 1963.

Newhall, Nancy. *P. H. Emerson: The Fight for Photography as a Fine Art*. Millerton, New York: Aperture, Inc., 1975.

Overland Monthly, 1900–1904. San Francisco: F. Marriott.

Peterson, Christian. "American Arts and Crafts: The Photograph Beautiful: 1895–1915." *History of Photography*, Vol. 16, No. 33, Autumn, 1992. London: Taylor & Francis, Ltd.

Photograms of the Year, 1901–1915. London: Dawbarn & Ward.

"News of Wedding Startles Society." *San Francisco Chronicle*, November 7, 1910.

The Professional Photographer, Vol. 71, p. 182, 1944. Rochester, New York: Eastman Kodak Co.

San Francisco Chronicle, Section CCC, p. 8, April 1, 1934.

San Francisco Examiner. Funeral Notice, July 16, 1957.

"San Francisco Man Perfects Photo Papers." *San Francisco Chronicle*, June 10, 1936.

"The San Francisco Salon." *Photo-Era*, Vol. 51, No. 6, 1923. Boston: Wilfred A. French

"The Second San Francisco Photographic Salon, Its Strong and Weak Points with a Criticism of Its Striking Features." *Camera Craft*, Vol. 4, No. 3, 1902.

Sierra Club Bulletin, 1900–1919. San Francisco: The Sierra Club.

Sterling, George. *Yosemite – An Ode*. San Francisco: A. M. Robertson, 1915.

Sunset (The Pacific Monthly), 1900–1920. San Francisco: The Southern Pacific Co.

Teiser, Ruth, and Catherine Harroun. "Conversations with Ansel Adams," Ansel Adams oral history conducted 1972, 1974, 1975; Regional Oral History Office, The Bancroft Library, University of California, Berkeley, 1978.

Taylor, Edward Robeson. *In the Keith Room at the Exposition*. San Francisco: Taylor & Taylor, 1915.

Treat, Archibald. "Important Lessons of the First Salon." *Camera Craft*, Vol. 2, No. 4, 1901.

Yochelson, Bonnie, and Kathleen Erwin. *Pictorialism into Modernism: The Clarence H. White School of Photography*. New York: Rizzoli International Publications, 1996.

Index

"A November Day," 17
Adams, Ansel, 9, 17, 25–27, 30, 32
Agfa, 24
Aiken, Charles Sedgewick, 15
Alameda Camera Club, 11
American Annual of Photography, 20, 31
"American Arts and Crafts: The Photograph Beautiful 1895–1915," 31
American Photography, 26
An Autobiography, 32
Andersen, Timothy J., 31
Ansel Adams: The Eloquent Light, 32
Ansco, 24
"Application of Artistic Principles to Photography," 14
Armer, Laura Adams, 11, 14
"The Art of Photography," 22
Arts and Crafts, 9, 15, 31
Arts & Crafts Guild of San Francisco, 31
"At Mission Santa Barbara," 17–18
Atkins, Henry, 31

Baker & Hamilton, 10
The Bancroft Library, 32
"Beach Grasses," 24
"Bell, Mission San Juan Capistrano," 20
Bennett, Jeanne E., 30
Bierce, Ambrose, 30
Birmingham, England, 24
Blanchard Gallery, 13
Blumann, Sigismund, 23, 32
Bohemian Club, 31
Boston, 24
Bridge of Allan, Scotland, 24
Brigman, Anne, 11, 15–16, 30–31
Brother Cornelius, 31
Burroughs, John, 9, 19, 30–31
"The Business of Photography," 22, 32

Cadanaso, Guiseppe, 30
California Camera Club, 9–14, 16, 22, 25, 27, 30
California Camera Club Exhibition of Industrial Arts, 12
California College of Arts & Crafts, 31
California Design 1910, 31
California the Beautiful, 21
"Calves," 11
The Camera, 28, 32
Camera Craft, 11–17, 20, 23, 24, 27, 30–32
Canada, 24, 26
Carbon Black, 32
Carlton, L. R., 32
Carmel, 15, 17, 20
Character Magazine, 9, 20
Charcoal Black, 9, 23–29, 32
Chicago, 14, 24
Clute, Fayette J., 16, 31
Coburn, Alvin Langdon, 9, 12–14, 30
"Conversations with Ansel Adams," 32
Coolbrith, Ina, 9, 18, 30–31
craftsman; craftsmen, 9, 14–15, 17–18, 20
The Craftsman, 15
Cummings, Blanche, 15
Cunningham, Imogen, 26

Dallas, 24
Danforth, Roy Harrison, 20, 31
d'Assonville, 10
Dassonville Competition, 26
Dassonville, Donald, 9, 23, 25, 28, 30–32
Dassonville, Frederick, 10, 16, 19, 24, 32
Dassonville, Georgia, 9
Dassonville, Gertrude, 19–20, 28
Dassonville, Marion, 9, 20, 28
Dassonville Photographic Paper Company, 23–24
Davie, Helen L., 30
Day, F. Holland, 12
"Day Dreams," 20
de Young Memorial Museum, 26
Defender, 24, 32
Demachy, Robert, 13
Department Var, 10
Depression, 26
Dixon, Maynard, 9, 15, 31
"Dome, Yosemite," 15
Dreier, Thomas, 9, 20
Dutch landscape, 12

Eastman Kodak, 24, 32
Edwards, John Paul, 22, 31
Eisen, Dr. E. G., 11
Elder, Paul, 12, 18, 21, 24, 30
Emerson, Peter Henry, 17
emulsion, 17, 22–26, 28
England, 9, 14
Ennis, Phillip, 23, 28, 32
Eugene, Frank, 12

Fairmont Hotel, 19
Father Anthony, 17
Father Francis, 17, 31
"Figure Study," 20
First American Photographic Salon, 14
"First American Salon," 30
First Los Angeles Photographic Salon, 12
First San Francisco Photographic Salon, 11, 17
Flood Building, 12
"For the Professional," 31
France, 10

Gamble, John, 15, 30
Gevaert, 24
Genthe, Arnold, 11, 13, 16, 30
Golden Gate Bridge, 27
Goudy, Frederic, 9–10, 30
Greene & Greene, 15
Greenway Ball, 19
Gribbes, Harry, 11
Group f/64, 24, 27
gumprint; gumbichromate print, 17

Hanscom, Adelaide, 14–15
Harmon, Edward N., 17
Harroun, Catherine, 32
Harte, Bret, 30
Hawaii Territorial Fair, 24
Hearn, Lafcadio, 31
Hill, Thomas, 15
Hirsch-Kayser Building, 16
Hispanic, 15
History of Photography, 31
Honolulu, 24
horoscope, 29
Hosmer, Harrie B.; H. B. Hosmer, 11
Hotel del Monte, 18
Hotel del Monte Art Gallery, 16
Hussey, Henry A., 22, 31

"Important Lessons of the First Salon," 12
"In the Art World," 18, 31
In the Keith Room at the Exposition, 21
"In the Land Fog," 11
"Individuality in Photography," 10, 12

Japanese, 15, 17, 24, 31
Jasper National Park, 26
Jerome, Lucy B., 18, 31
John Howell Books, 32
Jupiter, 29

Justinian & Caire, 23

Kansas City, 25
Kasebier, Gertrude, 13
Keith: Old Master of California, 31
Keith, William, 9, 15–20, 22, 26, 30–31
Keeler, Charles, 19

La Fayette Studio, 32
landscape, 9, 12–13, 15, 17–18
Lange, Professor Oscar V., 11
Lassen & Bien, 11
Lassen, Henry C., 12
Leica, 26
Lokke, Janet, 23, 30, 32
London, Jack, 30–31
Los Angeles, 13
"The Los Angeles Exhibition, Its History and Success and Those Responsible for It," 30

The Making of Forty Photographs, 30
"The Manipulation of Platinum Paper," 14, 30
Marin County, 17, 19
Mark Hopkins Institute, 11
Maurer, Oscar, 11–12, 14–15
Martinez, Xavier, 15, 31
Mechanics' Institute Pavilion, 12
Mechlin, Leila, 32
Mencken, H. K., 31
"The Metric System," 32
Mezey, Phiz, 29, 32
mission, 15, 17–18
modernism; modernist, 13
Monterey, 15–17
Monterey cypresses, 15
Moore, Eudorah M., 31

Morris, William, 14
"Morning Lights," 12
Mount Robson, 26
"Mount Tamalpais," 21
Muir, John, 9, 15, 20–21, 30
Murphy, Thomas G., 21

New Mexico, 26
New York, 14, 24, 28
New York Camera Club, 11
Newark Camera Club, 24, 32
Newark, New Jersey, 24
Newhall, Nancy, 25, 32
"No. 49 – Margaret," 13
Noskowiak, Sonya, 26

The Oakland Museum, 31
obituary, 29
The Old Spanish Missions of California, 18
Overland Monthly, 10, 30
Owens Valley, 27

Pacific Coast, 11, 17, 20
Palace of Fine Arts,
Palace of Liberal Arts, 20
Panama Pacific International Exposition, 20
Paris, 12, 31
patent, 13, 25
Paul Elder & Company, 14
Perry, Dr. and Mrs. E. E., 19
Perry, Gertrude Blanche, 19
Peterson, Christian, 31
Photo Era, 31
"Photographic Plates and Papers," 22, 32
Photographers' Association of California, 22
"Photography at the Exposition," 31
Photograms of the Year, 9, 16, 31

Photo-Secession, 12–14
pictorial, 9, 10, 12, 15, 17, 20, 24–27
Pitchford, Emily, 15
Pittsburgh, 24
"Platinotype Printing," 11
platinum emulsion; print; process, 14, 16–17, 20–24
Portland, 14, 24
"Portrait," 14
"Portrait of a Child," 15, 20
Power, Dr. H. D'Arcy, 11, 30
The Professional Photographer, 28

Redmond, Granville, 30
Reid, Charles K., 31
Richardson, Mary Curtis, 30
Ross [California], 19
Russ Building, , 24

Sachs Building, 20
Sacramento, 10, 17
Saint Francis Hotel, 14, 18
San Francisco Call, 18, 31
San Francisco Chronicle, 19, 27–28, 31–32
San Francisco Art Institute, 12
San Francisco earthquake, 16
"The San Francisco-Oakland Salon 1923," 31
Santa Barbara, 17–18
Second Annual Exhibition of the Guild of Arts and Crafts, 14, 30
Second San Francisco Salon, 12
Second San Francisco-Oakland Salon, 22
"The Second San Francisco Photographic Salon, Its Strong and Weak Points with a Criticism of Its Striking Features," 30
Sheppard, Morgan, 12
Sierra Club, 26

Sierra Club Bulletin, 21
Sierra Nevada, 10–11, 15, 17, 27
silver bromide; silver print, 22–24, 26
Smithsonian Institution, 27

Southern Pacific Railroad Company, 15, 17
Spanish-Mexican, 15
Stanford University, 29
Starr King Fraternity Second Annual Exhibition of Fine Art, 12
Steichen, Edward, 13
Sterling, George, 21, 31
Stieglitz, Alfred, 13, 16, 31
Strand, Paul, 26
Sunday Star [Washington DC], 27, 32
Sunset Magazine, 15, 21
Sunset Highways: A Book of Motor Rambles in California, 21

Taos Pueblo, 26, 32
Taylor, Edward Robeson, 21
Teiser, Ruth, 32
Telegraph Hill, 24
Teutonic, 16
Third San Francisco Photographic Salon, 13, 30
Tobey, Lilian W., 15, 31
Tomoye Press, 30
Toronto, 24
Torrey, Frederick, 31
Treasure Island, 27
Treat, Archibald, 12
Trinity School, 10
Truckee, 10

United States National Museum, 27

Van Dyke, Willard, 26

Vaponica tobacco, 16
Vickery, Atkins & Torrey, 16–17, 31
Vickery, W. K., 31

Washington, DC, 27
Weston, Edward, 26
White, Clarence H., 13
White Mountains, 27
Wightiana, Edith, 13
"W. E. Dassonville/Photographic Portraits in Platinum and Color," 31
Willis & Clement, 16–17
Winter, Robert W., 31
Wood, Elizabeth A., 10
Woods, Fred, 10
"Work in the Western States," 16
World's Fair, 27
World War I, 21

Yosemite, 14, 16–17
Yosemite: An Ode, 21, 31

Colophon

This edition of Dassonville is published in conjunction
with a traveling exhibition of William E. Dassonville's photographs
organized by Mills College Art Museum, 1999–2000.

The text and titles were composed in the Deepdene types,
designed in 1927 and 1928 by Frederic W. Goudy.
Design, typography and production was by
Richard D. Moore, Oakland, California.

Printed in Hong Kong through Acid Test Productions.